UNIQUE
Florida

A Guide to the State's Quirks, Charisma, and Character

Sarah Lovett

John Muir Publications
Santa Fe, New Mexico

Special thanks to Dixie Lee Nims, photo librarian, Florida Dept. of Commerce; W. Dean Sullivan, Florida Dept. of Commerce; Mary Ann Cleveland, State Library of Florida; Ted Keith, Florida D.E. M.; Alice Sealey, Tim Thompson, Abbie Casias, and Joan Morris, Florida State Archives.

John Muir Publications, P.O. Box 613, Santa Fe, NM 87504

Library of Congress Cataloging-in-Publication Data
Lovett, Sarah, 1953-
    Unique Florida : a guide to the state's quirks, charisma, and
character / Sarah Lovett.
        p.   cm.
    Includes index.
    ISBN 1-56261-104-6 : $10.95
    1. Florida—Guidebooks. 2. Florida—Miscellanea. I. Title.
    F309.3.L68 1993   93-3232
    917.5904'63—dc20   CIP

Design and Typography: Ken Wilson
Illustrations: Bette Brodsky
Typeface: Belwe, Oz Handicraft
Printer: Malloy Lithographing

Distributed to the book trade by
W. W. Norton & Co.
New York, New York

CONTENTS

INTRODUCTION

Nothing but perfect weather, endless shorelines, and theme parks—that's Florida, right? Splash on your sunscreen, sift sand through your toes, or watch trained dolphins jump through hoops, and you know you're in the Sunshine State. But, of course, there are many other things to discover about unique Florida. For instance, did you know that Florida is an important stop-over for migrating birds? And that you can stand anywhere in the state and never be more than 60 miles from tidewater? Did you ever imagine that Florida breweries produce award-winning beers? And that fishermen pull the world's largest bigmouth bass out of Florida's waters?

Unique Florida is a compilation of fascinating destinations, key facts, interesting charts, quick-reference maps, and fun trivia. Where else can you find a recipe for conch salad, a map of the state's wineries and breweries, a hurricane timeline, and a chart of eagle nesting sites?

You can open to any page and find readable, entertaining information. The index guides you to specific topics and sites. The contents is organized so that you can tell at a glance what subjects are covered in each section. However you choose to use this book, you'll soon discover what is unique about Florida. ⋐

The alligator is Florida's state reptile

Evolutionary Trivia

☛ Florida's oldest fossil, a turtle, hails from the Cretaceous period, 120 million years ago.

☛ The peninsula of Florida has probably been continually inhabited by humans for 10,000 years.

☛ Prehistoric Indians account for the longest period in Florida's human history.

The earth offers archaeologists a wealth of information about Florida's aboriginal cultures. "Middens" (shell and refuse heaps) and temple and burial mounds are scattered around the state. Unfortunately, commercial earth-moving equipment probably destroys one percent of the unexcavated sites each year. (For more on middens, see Spirit of Florida.)

An Indian mound near Poorman's Labor on the Ocklawaha River, 1892

Florida State Archives

FLORIDA

Population:
12,937,926

Area:
53,997 sq. miles

Capital:
Tallahassee

Nickname:
The Sunshine State

Date of Statehood: 1845 seceded, 1861 readmitted, 1868

Highest Elevation:
Lakewood, 345 feet

State Flower:
orange blossom

State Water Mammals:
manatee, dolphin

State Animal:
panther

State Shell: conch

State Song:
"Old Folks at Home"

THEN AND NOW

150 Million Years Ago–A.D. 1400

Florida State Archives

No Bones

Millions of years before humans evolved, dinosaurs ruled the Earth. The great beasts roamed the North American continent, but the area we now call Florida was blanketed by warm seas. Turtles, ancient whales and manatees, and shark-like creatures cruised the salty waters.

Over the eons, sedimentary layers of sand, marine shells, and limestone emerged from the sea to become a thumb jutting from the mainland's palm. Florida grew during the Great Ice Age when a massive volume of earth's water was claimed by glaciers. Flora and fauna took refuge from the frozen north and flourished in Florida's warmer climate. There was growing space for pine, oak, hickory, magnolia, palmetto, cypress, cabbage palm, pine, and mangrove in forests, swamps, and marshes. When great rains followed the Ice Age, many species of plants and animals lived and prospered on the "thumb." Saber-toothed tigers, mastodons, mammoths, giant bears, and wolves were among the four-legged beasts, and about that time the first humans also arrived. The fossils of these ancients are still discovered by construction crews and enterprising kids.

Familiar Florida—complete with recognizable beaches, lakes, plant life, animals—is a mere 6,000 years old. *FYI:* Florida Museum of Natural History, Gainesville; 904-392-1721. ☙

People

The same natural ingredients that give Florida its reputation as a vacation paradise undoubtedly attracted the earliest paleo-Indians. Ten or twelve thousand years ago the first migratory Indian groups probably reached Florida. But whether these ancient hunters traveled from the north or south is a matter of debate. Scholars who support the north-to-south theory believe hearty Asians crossed the Bering Strait about 20,000 years ago and journeyed toward warmer climes. Those who subscribe to the theory that early South and Central American residents migrated north base their belief on archaeological evidence demonstrating cultural commonalities between early Floridians and South and Central Americans. Whatever their path, paleo-Indians found a land overrun by bobcat, woolly bison, mastodon, mammoth, quail, duck, and goose, and a sea teeming with flounder, grouper, oyster, stone crab, and lobster—enough prey to make human predators skilled with flint points and atlatls believe they had found paradise. *FYI:* Museum of Archaeology, Fort Lauderdale; 305-925-7770; Crystal River Archaeological Site, Crystal River; 904-795-3817.

Florida State Archives

Timucuan, Tocobaga, Apalachee, Calusa, and Tequesta were some of the major tribes occupying Florida when the first European invaders arrived. These people fared badly during the period of coexistence that ultimately led to their extinction.

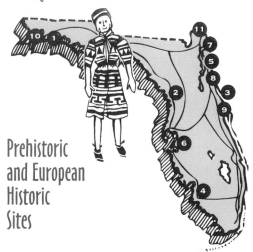

Prehistoric
and European
Historic
Sites

1400–1800s

1) Indian Temple Mound:
This was a government and
spiritual center for area vil-
lages. Remains of totems
and temples have been
excavated. *FYI:* Fort Walton;
904-243-6521.

**2) Crystal River State
Archaeological Site:** One
of Florida's premier pre-
Columbian sites; this was a
cultural center, occupied from 200 B.C. to A.D. 1400. The site includes
burial grounds, middens, and temple mounds. *FYI:* Crystal River;
904-795-3817.

3) Hontoon Island State Park: Indian mounds—one of snail shells,
the other of food—and a replica of a Timucuan Indian totem can be
viewed. *FYI:* via ferry.

4) Fort Myers Historical Museum: The area is rich with burial
mounds and middens, and the museum is located on the site of a
Calusa Indian settlement. *FYI:* Fort Myers; 813-332-5955.

5) Guana River State Park: Juan Ponce de León sailed on
Columbus's second expedition to the New World. After establishing an
outpost at Puerto Rico, Ponce de León went in search of a land where
the waters promised perpetual youth. In 1513, he arrived near what
would become the city of St. Augustine and claimed the land for
Spain. His landing place is believed to be located in this state park.
FYI: Ponte Vedra Beach; 904-825-5071.

6) De Soto National Memorial: Thirty-nine-year-old Hernando de
Soto arrived in Florida in 1539 to lead an expedition north from pre-
sent-day Tampa Bay. The handsome explorer led more than 600 sol-
diers, priests, servants, and slaves on a four-year quest that left De
Soto and half his group dead. The expedition is commemorated here.
FYI: Bradenton; 813-792-0458.

7) Fort Caroline National Memorial: French settlers (mostly
Huguenots) established this fort in 1564 in an effort to challenge
Spain's claim to the territory. *FYI:* Jacksonville; 904-641-7155.

8) St. Augustine: In 1565, Pedro Menendez de Aviles established the first permanent Spanish settlement here. Twenty-one years later, Sir Francis Drake led a British raid against the Spanish at St. Augustine, but it wasn't until the 1700s that the English began to look seriously at acquiring Florida territory. At the end of the Seven Years' War (1763), Florida became British. *FYI:* 904-829-5681.

9) Fort Matanzas National Monument: Here, in 1565, the Spanish under Menendez de Aviles defeated French Huguenots in a battle complicated by a hurricane. *Matanza* means "slaughter." *FYI:* south end of Anastasia Island; 904-471-0116.

10) Pensacola: The British divided Florida into east and west, and St. Augustine and Pensacola served respective provinces as capital cities. British engineer Elias Durnform designed a city plan in Pensacola that can be explored today in the Seville Square historic district. In 1781, Spain took control of Pensacola while the British were busy dealing with the American Revolution. *FYI:* 904-434-1234.

11) Fernandina Beach: The Louisiana Purchase left Spanish Florida surrounded by U.S. territory. Spain's protection of runaway slaves caused conflicts as American bounty hunters crossed the border hunting for escapees. This small town was the site of repeated skirmishes. *FYI:* on Amelia Island; 904-261-3248.

Florida State Archives

St. Augustine's oldest house

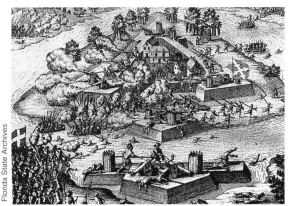

Florida State Archives

Menendez attacked French Huguenots at Fort Caroline on September 20, 1565

1400–1800s

Florida has more than 75 historical forts, many of them open to the public.

1) Fort Caroline National Memorial: The fort was established by French Huguenots in 1562. Reconstructed walls now stand on a nearby site. *FYI:* 904-641-7155.

2) Fort Clinch State Park: This was a battle site during the Civil War. The fort was also used as a training camp for Spanish Civil War volunteers. The first weekend of every month, fort staff recreate life in 1864. *FYI:* 904-277-7274.

3) Fort Foster: The fort has been restored and stands in Hillsborough River State Park. The original 1836 construction (known as Ft. Alabama) was built to supply army troops and protect the Hillsborough River crossing during the Second Seminole War. *FYI:* 813-986-1020.

4) Fort Christmas: Construction of this fort began on Christmas Day in 1837. Today, a replica of the fort houses a museum with military, Indian, and pioneer exhibits. *FYI:* 407-568-4149.

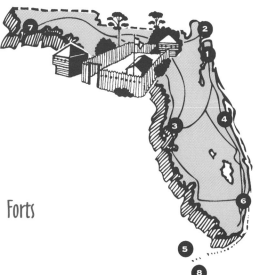

Forts

5) Fort Jefferson: In Dry Tortugas National Park, this spectacular 19th century fort—with hexagonal perimeter—was built by German and Irish crafts-men and American slaves. Federal troops occupied the fort throughout the Civil War. The "Lincoln Conspirators" (including Dr. Samuel Mudd, the doctor who innocently treated John Wilkes Booth after

President Lincoln's assassination) were sentenced to life imprisonment here. Mudd was eventually pardoned after he bravely treated 300 yellow fever victims during the 1867 epidemic. The fort was abandoned in 1867. *FYI:* By charter boat or plane. Primitive camping. U.S. Coast Guard, Key West; 305-247-6211.

6) Fort Lauderdale: A wooden fort—named after Maj. William Lauderdale—that stood here during the Seminole Wars rotted after it was abandoned in 1857. *FYI:* 305-463-4431.

7) Fort Barrancas: Restored by the National Park Service and administered by the Gulf Islands National Seashore. *FYI:* Pensacola, 904-455-5167.

8) Fort Zachary Taylor State Historic Site: The fort stands on the southwest tip of Key West and dates to the mid-1800s. *FYI:* 305-292-6713. 🐚

Juan Ponce de León (c. 1460-1521)

Ponce de León first saw the New World when he accompanied Cristóbol Colón on his second journey. After Ponce de León founded an outpost on Puerto Rico, the king of Spain offered him the governorship of Hispaniola. Before the explorer could seize the day, Diego Columbus (Christopher's son) usurped his claim. The king gave Ponce de León a second honor—the governorship of Bimini where youth-giving waters were said to flow. Real rewards awaited his discovery; land and gold were his for the taking in Bimini. Ponce de León spent a few weeks in the Bahamas before landing on the present-day continental United States. One "fountain of youth" can be visited at Ponce de León Springs State Recreation Area. *FYI:* NW Florida, 1/2 mile south of US90 on CR181-A; 904-836-4281.

Florida State Archives

1817–1868

Seminole Wars

The three Seminole Wars—the result of decades of white incursion into Seminole homeland—occurred between 1817 and 1859.

The Seminole Wars

1) Fort Gadsden State Historical Site: Built by British forces during the War of 1812, the fort was left to free blacks, escaped slaves, and Seminoles when the British departed. Known as the Negro Fort, Fort Gadsden was demolished by cannon fire during a siege in 1816 by General Jackson. *FYI:* 904-670-8988.

2) San Marcos de Apalache State Historic Site: General Jackson reentered Spanish territory in 1817 to arrest the Seminole chief, Neamathla. U.S. troops then seized this fort, and Jackson ordered the execution of British citizens suspected of inciting Seminole raids. This diplomatic crisis between Spain, Britain, and the U.S. marked the beginning of the First Seminole War. *FYI:* St. Augustine; 904-925-6216.

3) Dade Battlefield State Historic Site: Here, in 1835, Seminole warriors ambushed a column of 105 American soldiers under the command of Major Dade en route from Fort Brooke to Fort King. *FYI:* 904-793-4781.

4) Bulow Plantation Ruins State Historic Site: John Bulow's vast plantation was burned by Seminoles in 1836. Today, only foundations and ruins remain. *FYI:* 904-439-2219.

5) Fort Cooper State Park: The Second Seminole War was the longest and costliest Indian war in America's history. During a U.S. campaign against the Seminoles, Fort Cooper was the site of a two-week siege by Native Americans. *FYI:* 904-726-0315.

6) Fort Foster: After the Dade Massacre, the U.S. Army established Fort Foster to protect the river crossing. *FYI:* 813-987-6771.

7) Battle of Loxahatchee River: This battle was fought on January 1838 just north of West Palm Beach (in present-day Jonathan Dickinson State Park). *FYI:* 407-546-2771.

8) Paynes Creek State Historical Site: The Third Seminole War site of a Seminole ambush that killed two men at the Kennedy-Darling trading post. *FYI:* 813-375-4717.

9) Chokoloskee Island: A major offensive was launched by the U.S. Army in 1857. Seminoles ambushed and killed Capt. Parkhill and five volunteers. The end of the war was at hand, and within a few years, almost all remaining Seminoles were forcibly removed from Florida. *FYI:* A statue at the Florida Capitol commemorates the Chokoloskee battle. 🌿

General Andrew Jackson (1767-1845)

Florida's first territorial governor, Andrew Jackson was orphaned and began his military career at age 14. Jackson successfully defended New Orleans against the British, and became the hero of the War of 1812. In 1818, Jackson was sent to Alabama to quash Seminole uprisings. Against orders, he crossed the border into Spanish Florida. The resulting diplomatic hullabaloo did not dampen Jackson's career. He became the seventh president of the United States in 1828.

Florida State Archives

Florida State Archives

Osceola (1818-1838)

Although his great-grandfather was a Scotsman, Seminole leader Osceola rejected his white blood and led resistance against the treaties of 1832 and 1833 which demanded Indian removal from Florida. In December 1835, Osceola's warriors killed Indian agent Wiley Thompson. Osceola and his band resisted capture for several years. When he responded to a flag of truce in 1837, Osceola was imprisoned at Fort Moultrie, where he soon died.

Florida State Archives

The outcome of the Battle of Olustee—the only major Civil War battle fought completely within Florida's borders—was a solid Union defeat

1861–1865

Civil War

For more than half a century, Florida was the site of fierce civil war—between Seminole Indians and U.S. settlers and soldiers, then between Union and Confederate soldiers. When Florida became a state in 1845, almost half of its 66,500 residents were slaves. In 1854, the Kansas-Nebraska Act was introduced into Congress and spurred a bitter struggle between abolitionists and pro-slavery factions. Citizens of Florida, which had a slave-based economy, who dared criticize slavery were banished, even murdered. The conflict escalated; on January 10, 1861, a final vote for Florida's secession from the Union was passed 62 to 7. Although many Floridians opposed secession, once the vote was cast, they resolved themselves to war. In 1862, Confederate and Union soldiers marched into battle.

1) Fort Pickens: This star-shaped stronghold was one of three strategic forts—the others were Fort Barrancas and Fort McRee—at

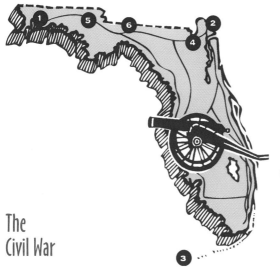

The Civil War

Pensacola. Federal forces took possession of Fort Pickens and began fortifications. The "Pickens Truce" orchestrated a stand-off between Union and Confederate troops. *FYI:* 904-934-2621.

2) Fort Clinch State Park: Confederates took over Fort Clinch— on Amelia Island—just prior to secession but were forced to withdraw soon after. *FYI:* 904-261-4212.

3) Fort Zachary Taylor State Historic Park: Union Capt. James Brannan refused to surrender this fort after secession, and it provided protection for Union ships in Key West harbor. *FYI:* 305-292-6713.

4) Battle of Olustee: Little fighting took place in Florida until 1864 and the Battle of Olustee. The outcome of the biggest battle—about 5,000 troops on each side—within Florida's borders was a decisive Confederate victory. The battle is reenacted here annually in February. *FYI:* 904-752-3866.

5) Battle of Marianna: In September 1864, this battle occurred when Federal forces marched on the town of Marianna. While Marianna's women and children found shelter in nearby Florida Caverns, townsmen mounted a defense but were outnumbered. The battle is reenacted each October. *FYI:* 904-482-9598.

6) Battle of Natural Bridge: This final major battle within Florida's borders was fought in 1865. Union forces intent on Tallahassee—the only capital east of the Mississippi River never to be taken by Union forces—began an inland march. Word reached the capital, and townspeople began constructing Fort Houston. Old men formed the Gadsden Greys, while boy cadets made up the "Baby Corps." With the help of these volunteers, Confederate troops forced Union soldiers to retreat. The victory was short-lived; within days, Gen. Robert E. Lee surrendered Confederate forces to Gen. Ulysses S. Grant. *FYI:* 904-925-6216. 🐚

Florida State Archives

Reconstruction politics and poll taxes gave blacks a less-than-equal voice in post-Civil War Florida

1870–1945

Post-Civil War Blues

As the nation struggled to recover from war, farmers, snowbirds, wealthy capitalists, entrepreneurs, and Cuban and Greek immigrants surged into Florida. Pulitzer Prize-winning novelist Marjorie Kinnan Rawlings wrote about the tough, courageous, and dirt-poor farmers—Florida Crackers—who pioneered northeastern Florida. At **Manatee Village Historical Park**, visitors can explore historic buildings including a church, courthouse, and 1912 Cracker home. *FYI:* Bradenton; 813-749-7165.

Cows have been big business in Florida for 100 years. Cracker cowboys at the turn of the century were similar to their Western brethren, except they had to deal with swamps, alligators, and swarming mosquitoes. Writer and illustrator Frederic Remington visited Florida in 1895 to research "Cracker Cowboys in Florida" for *Harper's Monthly*. Today, **Kissimmee Cow Camp** is the place for city slickers to kick up their heels. *FYI:* Lake Kissimmee State Park, Lake Wales; 813-696-1112.

Florida's first steam sawmill was built in 1841 near the state's lumber capital, Pensacola. Twelve years later the lumber industry was booming and Jacksonville boasted 14 mills. Post Civil War railroad expansion opened up new timber stands, and for a short time lumber was big business again. **Pensacola's North Hill Preservation District** is evidence of the turn-of-the-century timber industry heyday. By 1930, almost all Florida's best timber had been cut. *FYI:* Pensacola Chamber of Commerce; 904-438-4081. North Hill Preservation; 904-433-2329.

Florida's Key West "Conch" spongers first worked the sponge beds off the Keys in the 1890s. When competition between Conchs and Greek sponge divers became violent, Greek spongers moved north to **Tarpon Springs** where the industry thrived until the 1940s. You can still view sponge docks along Dodecanese Boulevard in Tarpon Springs, or take an excursion on **St. Nicholas Boat Line sponge boat**. *FYI:* 813-942-6425. 🐾

Cuban cigar manufacturers set up business in Key West after the failed Cuban revolution of 1868, but a hard-sell Tampa board of trade lured the hand-rolled cigar industry to the city.

In the 1870s Florida's coast was so remote, the government constructed houses of refuge where shipwrecked sailors could find safe haven. Gilbert's Bar House of Refuge, on Hutchinson Island, is the only remaining structure. It's also the oldest building in the area. *FYI*: 407-225-1875.

Most Americans had no idea of the real threat lurking off the coast of Florida (and much of the East Coast) when German U-boats cruised Atlantic and Gulf waters during the first six months of America's involvement in WW II. Germans sank almost 400 ships within sight of Florida's coast.

Florida Dept. of Commerce

Robert Overton, Florida Dept. of Commerce

Florida State Archives

Recent Times

Jacqueline Cochran (1910-1980)

Jacqueline Cochran never knew her real parents. She was raised by a poor family who scraped an existence from the company milltowns of Florida's panhandle. It was a simple and difficult beginning for a woman who would become one of America's most famous female flyers and test pilots and the first woman to break the sound barrier.

Within three days of her first flying lesson in 1932, Cochran soloed; three weeks later, she was a licensed pilot. When America entered WW II, she was appointed director of WASP (Women's Air Force Service Pilots). After the war, she set many jet-propulsion speed records over the California desert. Cochran received the International Flying Organization's gold medal for outstanding accomplishment in 1953.

Florida State Archives

Charles Kenzie Steele (1914-1980)

Civil rights leader C. K. Steele was a colleague of the late Martin Luther King, Jr., and he helped spearhead the national civil rights movement in the 1960s. Steele led a two-month bus boycott in Tallahassee, and he was successful in integrating lunch counters, airports, bus stations, and movie theaters. A one-time member of the Florida Human Relations Council, he also served as pastor of the Bethel Baptist Church in Tallahassee for almost thirty years. Steele was recognized for his contribution to civil rights by the National Association for the Advancement of Colored People (NAACP), and he was honored at the Southern Christian Leadership Conference in Cleveland in 1980. 🐚

Florida State Archives

Seminoles Today

By all estimates, only 200 to 300 Seminole Indians withstood relocation efforts. They formed the core of the state's present Seminole Indian population. Two language groups are represented: Muskogee-speaking Cow Creek Seminoles and Miccosukee.

The **Miccosukee Indian Village** west of Miami—tribally owned and operated—is one place to learn about Seminole culture. An airboat tour of a typical village, a museum, a restaurant, and arts and crafts demonstrations are all part of the package. *FYI:* on US41; 305-223-8380.

The **Seminole Cultural Center** (Tampa) and the **Fort Lauderdale Historical Society** (Fort Lauderdale) both have exhibits featuring traditional Seminole culture. *FYI:* Cultural Center, Orient Rd.; 813-623-3549; Historical Society, 2nd Ave.; 305-463-4431. ❧

Betty Mae Tiger Jumper

B orn in Indiantown in 1922, Betty Mae Tiger Jumper was the daughter of a white father and a Seminole mother. In the 1940s, she was one of the first Seminoles in Florida to graduate from high school. Her training as a nurse and her skills as a trilingual translator made her instrumental in bringing health care to the Seminole tribe. Jumper worked to organize the tribe in 1957; ten years later she became the first female tribal chairman. She also served many years as tribal public relations director and as editor of the *Seminole Tribune*. ❧

Space Shuttle Flight Program

T he first shuttle flights into space with reusable spacecraft were inaugurated on April 12, 1981. These craft—equipped with crews and equipment—are regularly launched from Cape Canaveral. Flights were temporarily halted in 1986 after the spacecraft Challenger exploded after liftoff, killing the seven astronauts on board. In 1988, shuttle flights resumed.

Florida Dept. of Commerce

Cape Canaveral

THE NATURAL WORLD

Florida Dept. of Commerce

Four geologic land-form regions—the Northwest Plateau and the Tallahassee Hills, the Central Highlands, the Coastal Lowlands, and the Southern Lowlands—roughly divide Florida. For the viewer, this translates into flat lands, rolling hills, flat woods, swamps, lakes, and sink-holes.

Building Florida

The term "Floridian Plateau" applies not only to the Florida "thumb" but to an equal or greater area covered by less than 300 feet of water. The Florida Keys mark the end of the plateau where it plunges into the Straits of Florida.

Hundreds of millions of years ago, the thumb consisted of a string of smoking volcanoes severed from the North American landmass by ocean. Those ancient volcanoes were buried by limestone sedimentary deposits for half a billion years; the limestone layers finally emerged from the ocean in the Late Tertiary.

The Ice Age gathered up ocean waters and left Florida twice as large as it is currently. The climate was rainy and cool—but much more hospitable than the ice-covered north. During the Pleistocene, great mastodons and saber-toothed tigers roamed the land.

As the Ice Age ended, melting and refreezing waters terraced the land. The climate became increasingly dry, and dunes formed. Today, Florida's landscape is still changing with the help of erosion, wind, rain, tides, and rivers—all doing their job to sculpt the earth. 🌿

Natural Trivia Quiz

1) The highest point in Florida—in the Panhandle—is ___ feet above sea level. **a)** 233 feet **b)** 1,021 feet **c)** 345 feet

2) The lowest point is _____. **a)** sea level **b)** 100 feet **c)** 21 feet

3) Florida ranks ___ in size in the United States. **a)** 15th **b)** 22nd **c)** 5th

4) Located 12 miles northwest of Brooksville, in Hernando County, you'll find the state's _____. **a)** Florida Divide **b)** oldest limestone formation **c)** geographic center

5) _____ is the nation's second-largest freshwater lake contained within the boundaries of a single state. **a)** Lake Okeechobee **b)** Lakeland **c)** Lake George

Answers: 1) c 2) a 3) b 4) c 5) a

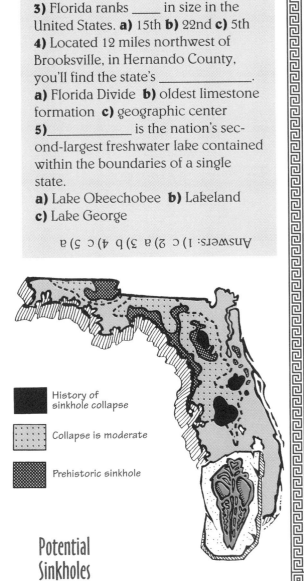

■ History of sinkhole collapse

▫ Collapse is moderate

▨ Prehistoric sinkhole

Potential Sinkholes

Down Below

Sinkholes are to Florida what mountains are to Colorado. Attracting visitors since the late 1800s, the 120-foot bowl-shaped sinkhole at **Devil's Millhopper State Geological Site** (Gainesville) was created when an underground limestone cap collapsed long ago. Fossil marine shells, shark's teeth, and the bones of extinct mammals have been excavated from the sink. *FYI:* 2 miles northwest of Gainesville on SR 232; 904-336-2008.

Falling Waters Sink—100 feet deep and 20 feet wide—is a cylindrical pit that boasts a 67-foot waterfall that disappears down the sink's "plug." **Falling Waters State Recreational Area** is known for its exceptional flora and geologic formations. *FYI:* 3 miles south of Chipley off SR 77A; 904-638-6130.

The endangered Florida panther is Florida's state animal

Jim Reed, Florida State Archives

Flora and Fauna

In Florida even indigenous plant and animal species seem exotic; some are found nowhere else in the contiguous United States. Florida panthers, miniature Key deer, manatees, and American crocodiles—all endangered species—have habitats restricted to the state. Egrets, ospreys, herons, kites, brown pelicans, woodpeckers, wood storks, vultures, and songbirds by the thousands spend the winter or the year here. Florida has more snake species than any other state, and six are poisonous: coral snakes, copperheads, cottonmouths, and pygmy, diamondback, and canebrake rattlesnakes. Less intimidating reptiles include gopher tortoises and five species of sea turtles (all threatened or endangered): leatherbacks, loggerheads, Atlantic greens, hawksbills, and Atlantic ridleys.

It's estimated that 115 native freshwater fish species swim in Florida's lakes and rivers, and an additional 175 marine and exotic species migrate into the streams. Almost one-half of the native freshwater species are found in or west of the Suwannee River system. The Apalachicola and Escambia rivers each contain more than 80 different species. Freshwater fish include black bass (tournaments for the world's largest are held regularly), catfish, shad, and sturgeon. Bonefish, barracuda, sailfish, bonita, marlin, and redfish are some of Florida's saltwater species.

Florida's incredibly diverse wildlife is facing the same problems that exist all over the world—human encroachment of habitats, introduction of exotic (and competing) species, overhunting, and pollution. ☙

Robert Overton, Florida Dept. of Commerce

The brown pelican is a Species of Special Concern in Florida

The manatee is unique to the state

Florida State Archives

Birding News

The eagle, America's national symbol of freedom, is doing well in Florida. Within the last 15 years, there have been almost 5,000 southern bald eagle hatchings. Florida eagle nesting territories have been expanded, and populations have stabilized since the first reliable counts in 1973.

Florida panthers and manatees are just two of the state's many endangered or threatened animals, or Species of Special Concern. Any citizen who witnesses a violation of Florida's wildlife laws should call, within Florida, "Wildlife Alert":
☞ Lakeland, 800-282-8002
☞ West Palm Beach, 800-432-2046
☞ Panama City, 800-342-1676
☞ Ocala, 800-342-9620
☞ Lake City, 800-342-8105

Eagle Nesting Sites, 1991

County	Number
Alachua	39
Citrus	6
Charlotte1	4
De Soto	2
Highlands	5
Hillsborough	11
Lake	23
Lee	21
Manatee	6
Marion	26
Pasco	4
Pinellas	10
Polk	46
Sarasota	12

Florida State Archives

Indigenous Torreya trees grow in Torreya State Park near Bristol and Greensboro

Biodiversity

The 18,000 acres included in **Payne's Prairie State Preserve** rank naturally and historically among Florida's most important. At least twenty unique biological communities are contained within the preserve, among them, pine flat woods, hammocks, swamp, pond, and wet prairie. This accounts for the amazing variety of animal species including sandhill cranes, eagles, hawks, wading birds, otters, and alligators. You can explore on foot, bicycle, or horseback; via sailboat, canoe, or electric powerboat; or take a ranger-guided nature walk (weekends only). *FYI:* 10 miles south of Gainesville; 904-466-4100 or 466-3397.

Ochlockonee River State Park preserves diverse habitats for gray foxes, deer, bobcats, and a profusion of bird species, including the threatened and endangered red-cockaded woodpecker. Wildlife study and fishing are specialties here. *FYI:* 4 miles south of Sopchoppy on US319; 904-962-2771.

At **Homosassa Springs State Wildlife Park** you'll see the easygoing and highly endangered Florida manatee as you walk underwater in the Spring of 10,000 Fish. Bobcats, alligators, a Florida black bear, crocodiles, and birds are part of the wildlife display and educational programs. The Animal Encounters Arena is where the state's reptiles show off. *FYI:* Homossassa Springs 75 miles north of Tampa; 904-628-2311.

Bugged

Mosquitoes, sandflies, chiggers, palmetto bugs (roaches), fleas, and ticks have as much to do with Florida's human history as humans do. Paleo-Indians, Seminole Indians, Spanish, French, and British residents all had to suffer the plague of tiny and not-so-tiny buzzing, biting, whizzing, and stinging animals. In fact, some failed settlers credited invertebrates with their downfall.

Diseases such as yellow fever, malaria, and encephalitis can be transmitted by mosquitoes, and many such plagues raged during Florida's history. These days, the medical profession offers protection against most mosquito-borne illnesses. Still, don't plan to venture into the backcountry or the wetlands without abundant protection, including appropriate clothing and insect repellent.

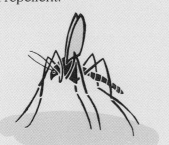

Florida's Wild Trivia

☛ Killer bees may invade Florida! It sounds like a tabloid headline, but it's a real source of worry for beekeepers. Honey-bees are no match for aggressive killer bees.

☛ Florida's black-legged ticks carry Lyme disease. Insect repellent is a must when visiting woodlands.

☛ Be on the lookout for four species of widow spiders native to Florida. Black, red, or brown—they're all very poisonous. The brown recluse spider (a.k.a. the fiddler or violin spider because that shape is outlined on its back) injects a prototoxin into its victim. Severe bites may take months to heal.

☛ Cottonmouth snakes—the only venemous water-dwelling snakes in North America—are named for the white interior of their mouth.

☛ Seven species of man-eating sharks (including the great white) have been known to cruise Florida's waters. Attacks are rare, but exercise caution when swimming.

Seminole Indians call the South Florida Everglades Pa-Hay-Okee, which translates as "grassy waters"

Everglades National Park and **Big Cypress National Preserve** consist of more than 2 million acres—just 20 percent of what was once a 50-mile-wide river flowing from Lake Okeechobee to Florida Bay and the Gulf of Mexico. Roughly 30 percent of South Florida's Everglades has been altered by agriculture and urban development, and another 50 percent has been modified to create Water Conservation Areas. Today, conflicting human demands for the water crucial to life in the Everglades threaten the survival of this unique ecosystem.

A blend of tropical and temperate species has earned the Everglades ecosystem its designation as an International Biosphere Reserve and a World Heritage Site. Ospreys, wood storks, crocodiles, green sea turtles, great white herons, southern bald eagles, and manatees all find refuge here. The subtropical climate governs life in the Everglades. Although the weather seems uniform, there are two distinct seasons: summer, which is wet, and winter, which is dry. Precipitation can exceed 50 inches a year, and humid conditions mean an abundance of mosquitoes and other insects. They are crucial to intricate food webs; you are not, so bring repellent, sunscreen, and appropriate clothing.

FYI: Everglades National Park; restricted camping, fishing, bicycling, hiking, tours; main visitor center on Route 9336, 10 miles southwest of Florida City; park headquarters: 305-242-7700; Shark Valley: 305-221-8776; Flamingo: 305-253-2241; Everglades City: 813-695-3311.

FYI: Big Cypress National Preserve; hiking, picnicking, primitive camping; via Route 41 between Shark Valley and Everglades City; 813-695-2000 or 813-695-4111. 🐚

Marjory Stoneman Douglas (b. 1890)

Conservationist Marjory Stoneman Douglas moved to Florida in 1915, fifty years before she would become the foremost champion of the Everglades. After graduating from Wellesley in 1912, she was married briefly to Kenneth Douglas, then relocated to Miami and began working for her father, Frank Stoneman, who had started the newspaper that became the *Herald.* In 1924, she left the newspaper business to become a full-time freelance writer; eventually that led to a contract to write *The Everglades: River of Grass.* The landmark book appeared in 1947—with its message that the Everglades were dying due to human violation—and it changed the popular perception of that fragile ecosystem. In 1970 she founded the nonprofit lobby Friends of the Everglades. The group fought successfully for the rediversion of the Kissimmee River (authorized by Washington in 1984) so it would once again nourish marshlands, as well as the creation of a 35,000-acre marshland below Lake Okeechobee to cleanse agrichemicals from south-flowing water. In 1992—at the age of 101—Douglas was still fighting for her "river of grass."

Florida State Archives

At **Collier-Seminole State Park**—where Big Cypress meets the Everglades—more than 6,000 acres of salt marshland and tropical hardwood hammock shelter a wealth of rare plant and animal species. The threatened and endangered species include the royal palm, brown pelicans, red-cockaded woodpeckers, manatees, Florida black bears, and Florida panthers. The park is situated just west of Marco Island. Boat tours, canoeing, primitive camping, and fishing are permitted in some areas. *FYI:* 17 miles south of Naples; 813-394-3397.

Florida Keys

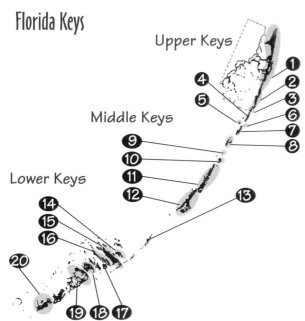

Upper Keys

Middle Keys

Lower Keys

Upper Keys

1) Key Largo: This Key is best known for **John Pennekamp Coral Reef State Park**, the nation's first sub-aquatic state park. It covers roughly 70 nautical square miles and is designed to preserve part of the only living coral reef in the U.S. *FYI:* north of Key Largo; 305-451-1202.

2) Plantation Key: This was Calusa Indian territory centuries ago. Today, the Plantation Yacht Harbor Resort and Marker 88 restaurant provide entertainment for those who seek it.

3) Windley Key: The gigantic resort of Holiday Isle dominates the Key.

4) Upper Matecumbe Key: The hurricane of 1935 devastated this Key and left a lone grave marker standing. You can see it on the grounds of the Cheeca Lodge.

5) Lignumvitae Key: This 345-acre island shelters the last virgin tropical forest in the Keys. Lignumvitae escaped dynamiting and development, the pattern in these islands. The lignum vitae is a tree that was described in the fifteenth century as growing in the Garden of Eden.

6) Indian Key: Boat to **Indian Key State Historic Site** and navigate above the most treacherous reefs off the Florida coast. Jacob Housman bought Indian Key in 1831 as headquarters for his salvaging business. It prospered until 1840 when Seminole Indians retaliated against Housman's hostilities and burned much of the settlement. *FYI:* 305-664-4815.

7) Lower Matecumbe Key: Picnic along the lovely stretch of water between Lower Matecumbe and Craig Key and watch for pelicans, herons, ibises, and egrets.

8) Long Key: Primitive camping is available at **Long Key State Recreation Area**, where nature trails let you explore tropical hammocks. *FYI:* 305-664-4815.

Middle Keys

9) Conch Key: This is all of 16 acres inhabited by retirees, fishermen, and lobstermen.

10) Duck Key: This is the site of Hawk's Cay Resort, which offers luxury in the Middle Keys.

11) Grassy Key: Mitzi, the dolphin of "Flipper" fame, is buried here. There's also a Dolphin Research Center.

12) Key Vaca: The town of Marathon takes up almost all of Key Vaca. Sombrero Beach provides the best swimming. Crane Point Hammock—a 64-acre tropical forest—offers a break from town.

13) Bahia Honda Key: The swimming on "Deep Bay" Key is excellent, unlike most of the Florida Keys. Beach dune, mangrove forest, coastal berm, tropical hardwood hammock, and submerged marine habitats are all biocommunities within **Bahia Honda State Park**. *FYI:* 305-872-2353.

Lower Keys

14) No Name Key: Cuban refugee guerrilla fighters trained here in the 1960s. There's no electricity and few residents, but there are many deer. The No Name Pub serves good pizza.

15) Big Pine Key: This island is known for its tiny Key deer, which stand a mere 2 1/2 feet tall and weigh about 70 pounds. A Key deer fawn leaves a hoofprint the size of a fingernail. These animals survived near-extinction from overhunting with the help of environmentalist and refuge manager Jack Watson.

16) The Torch Keys: Little, Middle, and Big Torch keys were named for the resinous torchwood trees that grow here.

17) Ramrod Key: Looe Key—miles offshore from Ramrod Key—is a National Marine Sanctuary and one of the most spectacular reefs in the Keys; great snorkeling and diving but no collecting.

18) Cudjoe Key: The crayfish have a reputation here, and Fat Albert—a ground-tethered radar blimp—keeps an eye on things.

19) Sugarloaf Key: A sponge-raising venture was started here at the turn of the century by Charles Chase. When Chase went bankrupt, he sold most of Sugarloaf to R. C. Perky, a real estate salesman. Perky was responsible for the bat tower—a bat condo designed by Dr. Charles Campbell—which seems destined to stand eternally batless.

20) Key West: This island lies 45 miles north of the Tropic of Cancer, and it's the end of the line as far as Keys are concerned. Sloppy Joe's Bar and Hemingway's house are among the attractions that draw a million visitors every year.

Weather the Weather

Florida license plates promote the "Sunshine State," and no one would argue that climate is a crucial part of the state's economy. When it's slick, slushy, and sub-zero in other parts of the country, Florida remains balmy, one of the warmest spots on the mainland. Tourists who flee northern climes—sometimes referred to as "snow-birds"—are indignant if they don't have the option of a second-degree Florida sunburn.

Heating Up

Florida's tropical clime may get even warmer—if current pollution trends continue to add to the greenhouse effect. Scientists estimate that global warming of just a few degrees could melt portions of the polar ice caps and raise ocean levels by about 15 feet. For Florida, that could mean wetter summers, warmer temperatures, more flooding, fewer wetlands, and a loss of up to a quarter of its landmass (the shaded part of the map). Fish, mangroves, and the citrus industry could all migrate north. Certain fish species off the state's coasts would likely either die or move to cooler waters. 🦐

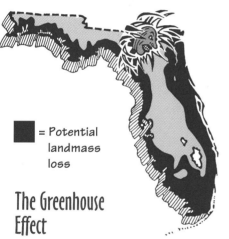

■ = Potential landmass loss

The Greenhouse Effect

Weather Trivia Quiz

1) On Florida's southern peninsula, prevailing winds blow _____ and _____.
a) west and southwest **b)** southeast and east **c)** up and down
2) Florida and New Mexico have _____ in common.
a) seasonal lows **b)** annual precipitation rates **c)** frequent thunderstorms and a high proportion of deaths by lightning
3) Florida's greatest recorded snowfall was _____ inches, measured in 1899 at Lake Butler.
a) 40 inches **b)** 4 inches **c)** 1/4 inch

Answers: 1) b 2) c 3) b

Dr. John Gorrie (1802–1855)

John Gorrie, an illegitimate child, was born in 1802 in the West Indies. His mother, a governess, brought him to South Carolina when he was a year old. Gorrie graduated in 1827 from the New York College of Physicians and Surgeons. Traveling with his mother, he moved to Sneads, Florida (on the Apalachicola River), in 1831.

Gorrie—the father of air-conditioning and refrigeration—just wanted his patients (chiefly, victims of yellow fever and malaria in the cotton port of Apalachicola) to be cool. He theorized that patients who were cool and dry would have much better odds of recovering from disease. The deadly fevers were linked with hot, humid environments and never existed in cold, dry climates. (At the time, no one believed the mosquito was a carrier of fever.) In the process of cooling his patient's rooms, Gorrie invented a miracle machine capable of manufacturing artificial ice.

Gorrie's first experiment consisted of ice suspended over pipes leading to and from a hospital room. Later—after refinements that included compressor pumps and a steam engine—the doctor made ice. Patents were issued in 1851, but they expired twenty years later unimproved because Gorrie had used up all his money. Ice shippers may be most to blame for Gorrie's lack of success in producing his air-conditioner. Fearing competition in a very lucrative market, the shippers did their best to ridicule Gorrie. The doctor died in 1899, a discouraged man. Twelve years after his death, his statue was placed in the Statuary Hall in the Capitol at Washington. *FYI:* a replica of Gorrie's ice-making machine is on display in the John Gorrie State Museum, Apalachicola; 904-653-9347.

Florida State Archives

Florida State Archives

Miami and the aftermath of the 1926 hurricane

Hurricane Heavies

They're known as willy-willy's in Australia, cyclones in the Indian Ocean region, typhoons in the Pacific Ocean, and baguils in the Philippines. But Florida and hurricanes (the word stems from *huracan*, a Native American word meaning "evil spirit") go together. The Sunshine State lies in the path of tropical storms that are born in the Caribbean Sea or the Atlantic Ocean east of the Lesser Antilles. The season is basically short—August through October—but it can be memorably violent. 🐚

Hurricane Trivia Quiz

1) A hurricane is a tropical storm that reaches winds of ____ miles per hour.
   a) 55 **b)** 74 **c)** 100

2) A tropical storm is a counterclockwise cloud circulation with winds from ____ to ____ miles per hour.
   a) 30 , 73 **b)** 45 , 50 **c)** 74, 90

3) A tropical depression is a low pressure area with rotary circulation of clouds and winds up to ____ miles per hour.
   a) 26 **b)** 29 **c)** 38

4) A Category 1 hurricane has winds reaching speeds of ___ to ___ miles per hour.
   a) 24, 36 **b)** 74, 95 **c)** 96, 105

5) A Category 5 hurricane has winds reaching speeds of more than ___ miles per hour.
   a) 100 **b)** 110 **c)** 155

6) Built by Hungarian Ferenc Varga, a monument to victims of the ____ hurricane stands in Bell Glade.
   a) 1901 **b)** 1229 **c)** 1928

7) A monument to the ____ victims of the 1935 hurricane can be seen in Islamorodo, Mile Marker 81.5.
   a) 200 **b)** 423 **c)** 609

Answers: 1) b 2) a 3) c 4) b 5) c 6) c 7) b

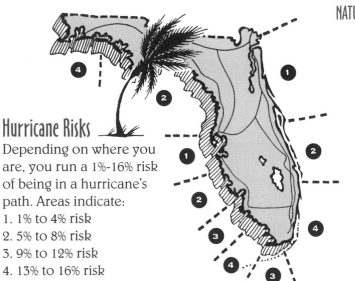

Hurricane Risks

Depending on where you are, you run a 1%-16% risk of being in a hurricane's path. Areas indicate:
1. 1% to 4% risk
2. 5% to 8% risk
3. 9% to 12% risk
4. 13% to 16% risk

HURRICANE TIMELINE

☛ 1559: Tristan de Luna lands at Pensacola Bay during a hurricane.

☛ 1565: A hurricane aids Menendez de Aviles in his defeat of French Huguenots.

☛ 1622: Spanish treasure ships—Nuestra de Atocha and Santa Margarita—sink during a hurricane.

☛ 1750s: The European settlement on Santa Rosa Island is destroyed by a hurricane.

☛ 1848: An anonymous hurricane destroys Fort Brooke in the Tampa Bay area.

☛ 1896: More than 100 people die and 7 million dollars' worth of damage is caused.

☛ 1926: Roughly 400 people are killed and thousands of dollars worth of structural damage is caused by a hurricane.

☛ 1928: Lake Okeechobee overflows its banks and 2,200 people drown because of a hurricane; the levees you see today were built following the devastation.

☛ 1935, Labor Day: A hurricane destroys the Flagler Overseas Railroad when winds top 200 mph; a barometer reading of 26.35 is one of the lowest pressures recorded in the Western Hemisphere.

☛ 1945: Property losses top $30 million.

☛ 1964: Hurricane Cleo leaves $128 million in damages in its wake.

☛ 1985: Eleven named storms blow out of the Atlantic and the Gulf.

☛ 1992: The costliest natural disaster in the U.S., Andrew causes damages exceeding $20 billion.

GOING TO TOWN

Florida State Archives, Fishbaugh Collection

During the Florida Land Boom, special buses carted prospective buyers from Miami to Coral Gables

Land Boom

Thousands of years before terms such as "tourist" or "land rush" were coined, humans were gathering in this warm, sunny region. Over the centuries, people continued to flock to Florida—Seminoles, Spaniards, French, British, and Americans. But the Great Florida Land Boom (1921-1926) was something new. Never before had people rushed into the state by the tens of thousands as land prices soared, mostly due to the huckster's artful dodge. Land parcels offered to Northern marks were located only a skip and a jump from towns that didn't exist. People who couldn't afford to speculate were losing their shirts and their dollars—so much so that Ohio passed "blue sky" laws forbidding the sale of Florida's land within Ohio's borders. Illinois and Minnesota publicly warned citizens not to be bamboozled by the artificially produced land boom.

Still, the buying frenzy showed no sign of tapering off. Coral Gables, Hollywood-by-the-Sea, and Tampa's water-logged Davis Islands were part of the scam. In Sarasota, Fort Myers, St. Petersburg, and Tampa, land prices soared from $50 an acre to $10,000 dollars an acre. When the inevitable bust occurred, at least 150 new towns suffered hard financial times, and 1926 was marked by a bona fide "crash." But the boom was the genesis of many new towns. 🐚

Florida Dept. of Commerce

Miami Beach today

Miami & Miami Beach

Pop. 358,548
Elev. 5 ft.
Noted for: cruise ships, hustle, glamour, sunburn, architecture, food, music, Metrozoo, Miami Seaquarium, Latin cultures
Nearby: Vizcaya Museum and Gardens, Museum of Science and Space Transit Planetarium, Big Cypress National Preserve, Everglades National Park, Miccosukee Indian Village and Airboat Rides
Convention & Visitors Bureau: 305-539-3000

Miami was settled in 1870 but remained a fishing village until railroad magnate and developer Henry Morrison Flagler arrived with his Florida East Coast Railway in 1896. Growth proceeded at a steady pace until the 1920s boom brought 25,000 realtors to town. In 1925, downtown Miami was going at $20,000 a front foot, and total construction topped $100 million. The balloon burst during the devastating 1926 hurricane, and the Great Depression stole the rest of Miami's air until WW II sparked new growth. Since the 1940s, Miami's steady growth has been based on year-round tourism, international commerce and trade, and industry and agriculture. Today, Miami is home to so many Cubans and Latin American political refugees, it is sometimes called "the capital of Latin America."

Special Events in Miami

December - January
Orange Bowl Festival
Taste of the Grove: two-day food festival in Coconut Grove

February
Coconut Grove Arts Festival
Doral Ryder Open PGA golf tournament

March
Carnaval Miami: nation's largest Hispanic culture festival includes Carnaval Night, the Paseo parade, and the Calle Ocho Festival in Little Havana.
Italian Renaissance Festival

April
Grand Prix Miami

June
Miami/Budweiser Unlimited Hydroplane Regatta

December
Miccosukee Indian Arts Festival

St. Augustine

Pop. 11,692
Elev. 6 ft.
Noted for: Spanish architecture, Spanish quarter (including the Gomez house and the functioning blacksmith shop), Castillo de San Marcos National Monument, Mission of Nombre de Dios, Lightner Museum, Lighthouse Museum of St. Augustine, Flagler College, Fountain of Youth
Nearby: Anastasia State Recreation Area, St. Augustine Alligator Farm
St. Augustine Chamber of Commerce: 904-829-5681

Florida State Archives,

St. Augustine may be the oldest permanent settlement in the U.S

St. Augustine was under Spanish rule longer than it has been under the Stars and Stripes, and it still retains some of the feel of a European city. St. Augustine's Spanish history began on September 8, 1565, when Don Pedro Menendez de Aviles dropped anchor off the mainland and rowed to shore.

More recently, in the 1880s, St. Augustine became a fashionable resort when Henry Morrison Flagler constructed two great hotels, and the city became headquarters of the Florida East Coast Railroad. Although the railroad still has its headquarters here, the city's economy includes seafood processing, farming, boat-building, printing and bookbinding, and aircraft manufacturing.

Special Events in St. Augustine

April
  St. Augustine Easter Festival
    Beaches Spring Festival
June
  Cross and Sword (official state play)
  Spanish Night Watch
December
  St. Augustine Christmas Parade

Pensacola

Pop. 58,165
Elev. 11 ft.
Noted for: Naval Air Station (including the National Museum of Naval Aviation, the USS Lexington, Fort Barrancas, and the Old Pensacola Lighthouse), Seville Square Historic District, Pensacola Museum of Art, St. Michael's Cemetery, Old Christ Church, the Barcley House
Nearby: Gulf Islands National Seashore, shipwrecks (including the battleship USS Massachusetts) for scuba divers, freshwater and saltwater sports fishing
Visitor Information Center: 904-434-1234 or 800-343-432; out of state, 800-874-1234

Florida Dept. of Commerce

Pensacola Beach

Pensacola was first settled in 1752 after a hurricane wiped out an older community on Santa Rosa Island. Set on the edge of the great North American interior wilderness, the settlement was a major Indian trading center. The early mix of Scottish, Spanish, French, and British settlers, as well as free blacks, gave Pensacola a unique atmosphere. Today, the city still reflects its multicultural origins.

Special Events in Pensacola

April
  Pensacola Jazz Fest
June
  Fiesta of Five Flags—five different flags have flown over the city
September
  Pensacola Seafood Festival
November
  Greater Gulf Coast Arts Festival

Tallahassee

Pop. 124,773
Elev. 190 ft.

Noted for: historic Capitol-state building (now a museum), state capitol, Governor's Mansion, First Presbyterian Church (Florida's oldest public building in continual use), Florida State University, Museum of Florida History
Nearby: San Marcos de Apalachee State Historic Site, St. Mark's National Wildlife Refuge, Edward Ball Wakulla Springs State Park, Natural Bridge State Historic Site
Chamber of Commerce: 904-224-8116

Florida's capital city was founded in 1824 and still evokes plantation days. During the Civil War it was the only Confederate capital east of

the Mississippi that wasn't captured by Union forces. Now, Tallahassee's economy is organized around state and local government, lumber and wood production, food production, and the printing and publishing business.

Florida Dept. of Commerce

Historic areas of Tallahassee include the **Calhoun Street Historic District,** *the* **Brokaw-McDougall House,** *the* **Governor's Mansion,** *and the* **McGinnis-Munroe House**

Special Events in Tallahassee

March
  Natural Bridge Battle Reenactment
April
  Flying High Circus
  Springtime Tallahassee
  Spring Farm Days
July
  Summer Swamp Stomp: bluegrass, folk, and saltwater music
October
  North Florida Fair: exhibits, fairgrounds, midway
December
  December on the Farm: syrup making and other 1880s farm activities

Fort Lauderdale

Pop. 153,256
Elev. 15 ft.
Noted for: New York Yankees spring training, Bonnet House estate and plantation of artists Frederic and Evelyn Bartlett, Broward Center for the Performing Arts, Buehler Planetarium, Butterfly World, Discovery Center children's museum, Fort Lauderdale Swap Shop flea market, Davie Pro Rodeo, Dania Jai Alai, Flamingo Garden, Everglades Holiday Park, Riverwalk, Port Lauderdale, Museum of Art, Stranahan House
Nearby: Sawgrass Recreation Area, Ski Rixen water ski cableway, C. B. Smith Park, Pompano Harness Track, Seminole Indian Bingo
Fort Lauderdale Convention & Visitors Bureau: 305-765-4466

During the Seminole Wars a wooden fort was constructed here in what was swampland. The fort was named after Tennessee volunteer Maj. William Lauderdale. The fort eventually decayed, and the next significant building was a House of Refuge for shipwrecked sailors. When Frank Stranahan arrived in Fort Lauderdale in 1893, the town was a camp on the banks of the New River. Stranahan established a trading post for Seminoles and pioneers at the turn of the century. But it was Henry Flagler's railroad that really brought change, and Fort Lauderdale was incorporated in 1911.

In more recent history, Fort Lauderdale has earned a reputation as a Spring Break watering hole. "Where the Boys Are" sung by Connie Francis immortalized "The Strip," a beachfront stretch designed for cruising. But Fort Lauderdale seems to be maturing as a city, and Daytona Beach is providing competition for the college set.

Special Events in Ft. Lauderdale

January
Deerfield Beach Festival of the Arts
UNICEF World Peace Exhibition
Irishfest
February
Seminole Indian Tribal Festival
April
New River Jazz Festival
South Florida Black Film Festival
May
Medieval Festival

June
Goombay Festival
July
Sun-Sentinel Sandblast
October
Viva Broward, Latin Heritage Festival

Florida Dept. of Commerce

Panhandle Beaches

Panama City

Pop. 34,378
Elev. 29 ft.
Noted for: fishing, beaches, Miracle Strip Amusement Park, Gulfworld, glass-bottom boats, Junior Museum of Bay County, Museum of Man and the Sea, Ocean Opry
Nearby: Shell Island (accessible by boat), St. Andrews State Recreation Area, Eden State Gardens
Convention & Visitors Bureau: 904-233-6503; out of state, 800-722-3224
Chamber of Commerce: 904-785-5206
Panama City Beach Chamber of Commerce: 904-234-3193 (beach tourist info)

What's in a Name?
If you draw a line from Chicago to the Canal Zone's Panama City, you'd pass right through Panama City—Panama City, Florida. During the construction of both the Panama Canal and the Florida municipality, a developer was inspired by such thoughts when he decided on the name.

World War II kept Panama City bustling as factory workers migrated north to south by the thousands to find work in manufacturing and assembling munitions and ships. Today, Panama City is touted as the "resort capital of the panhandle," famous for its sugar-white beaches, clear water, and hustle-bustle.

Special Events in Panama City

April
  Offshore Power Boat Race Classic
May
  Spring Festival of the Arts
  Gulf Coast Triathalon
October
  Annual Indian Summer Seafood Festival
November
  Downtown Christmas Boat Parade of Lights
December
  Christmas Parade

St. Petersburg

Pop. 238,629
Elev. 44 ft.
Noted For: beaches, parks, yacht basins, Tampa Bay
Nearby: resort islands
Chamber of Commerce: 813-821-4069

St. Petersburg—Florida's fourth largest city—hosts more than one million visitors each year. Tourists come for sun, of course, especially as it shines over golf courses and boating opportunities. Although it's a tourist mecca, St. Petersburg is more traditional, more stately, quieter, and less glitzy than Miami and surrounds.

Special Events in St. Petersburg

March-April
  Festival of States
May
  Mainsail Sidewalk
  Arts Show
June
  Taste of Pinellas
  (food fest)
December
  Christmas in the Park
  with Santa Parade
  Lighted Boat Parade

Robert Overton, Florida Dept. of Commerce

St. Petersburg Municipal Pier today

Key West

Pop. 24,832
Elev. 5 ft.
Noted for: fishing, reef cruises, Conch-style architecture, Ernest Hemingway Home and Museum, Sloppy Joe's Bar, Audubon House and Gardens, Key West Aquarium, Wrecker's Museum, East Martello Gallery and Museum, Key West Lighthouse Museum
Nearby: Fort Jefferson National Monument
Chamber of Commerce: 305-294-2587

Key West, 1838

Ponce de León may have been the first European to spot Key West, but Native Americans had long been doing trade or battle here. This southernmost city in the continental U.S. is located on the last inhabited island in the Florida Keys. In 1890, it was Florida's largest city, when salvaging the cargo of ships wrecked on the reef was big business. During the past century, cigar making, sponge gathering, turtling, fishing, and shrimping have all been part of local island economy. These days, prosperity is synonymous with tourism.

Native islanders are known as "Conchs," and they are descendants of English loyalists who sought refuge after the American Revolution.

The gracious antebellum **Audubon House**—home of sea captain and wrecker John Geiger—contains a collection of 18th- and 19th-century furnishings that were here when Audubon visited the island to sketch and hunt. Original engravings by Audubon are on display. *FYI:* 205 Whitehead St.; 305-294-2116.

The **Ernest Hemingway Home and Museum** is a Spanish Colonial-style house purchased by the writer in 1931. Original furnishings and memorabilia make this a must for bibliophiles. Many of the trees and shrubs in the garden were planted by Hemingway. *FYI:* 907 Whitehead St.; 305-294-1575.

Orlando

Pop. 164,693
Elev. 106 ft.
Noted for: Leu Botanical Gardens, Lock Haven Park (including the Orlando Museum of Art and the Orlando Science Center), Church Street Station, Church Street Market
Nearby: Kennedy Space Center, Walt Disney World, Sea World of Florida, Universal Studios Florida, Wet 'n Wild
Orlando/Orange County Convention & Visitors Bureau:
407-363-5871

Orlando served as an encampment for soldiers during the Seminole War of 1835-1842 and as a trading post until 1857. Between the coming of the railroad from Sanford in 1880 and the establishment of the Kennedy Space Center to the southeast after WW II, Orlando has done nothing but grow.

Orlando is a hub for travelers on their way to Walt Disney World and other theme parks in the area. Those who spend time in the city will discover its abundance of lakes—54, in fact—as well as its parklike atmosphere. Aerospace, defense, the electronics industries, and a Navy recruit training center all keep Orlando's economy active.

Special Events in Orlando

January
  Florida Citrus Sports Holiday: Florida Citrus Bowl football game
    caps the month-long activities.
  Orlando Scottish Highland Games: pipe band competition,
    athletic events, Highland dancing, haggis hurling, Scottish food
February-March
  Central Florida Fair: horse shows, midway, entertainment
  The Nestle Invitational: Bay Hill Golf & Country Club, PGA
    tournamen
October
  Pioneer Days Folk Festival: sugarcane grinding, syrup making,
    crafts, bluegrass music, and clogging

Florida Dept. of Commerce

Fort Myers was the winter home of Thomas Alva Edison for more than forty years

Gainesville: Settled in 1830 as Hogtown, Gainesville today is a university city of almost 85,000 people. **Known for:** hunting and fishing in the area; the University of Florida; Florida Museum of Natural History; Kanapaha Botanical Gardens; Marjorie Kinnan Rawlings State Historic Site; Devil's Millhopper State Geological Site. **Alachua County Visitors & Convention Bureau:** 904-374-5231 ✆

Robert Overton, Florida Dept. of Commerce

Tampa Bay Sunshine Skyway

Lakeland: Named for the 13 lakes within the city's limits, Lakeland is located in Central Florida where citrus groves, packing, and processing provide much of the local economy. **Known for:** Florida Southern College (and the largest group of buildings designed by Frank Lloyd Wright); Polk Museum of Art; Orange Cup Regatta. **Chamber of Commerce:** 813-688-8551

Florida Dept. of Commerce

Bay Front, Sarasota

Jacksonville: It used to be an industrial, maritime Southern city, but now skyscrapers and white sands have refurbished Jacksonville's more modern self-image. **Known for:** the Riverwalk; Jacksonville Landing (festival marketplace); Jacksonville Zoological Park; Cummer Gallery of Art and Gardens; Jacksonville Art Museum; Jacksonville University; Kingsley Plantation State Historic Site. **Chamber of Commerce:** 904-366-6600

Tampa Convention and Visitors Bureau

Tampa's Bayshore Blvd. is filled with floats during the annual Gasparilla Parade

Town Trivia Quiz

1) _____ (next to Lake Okeechobee's shore) bills itself as "the sweetest town in the USA" because of its very close ties to the sugar industry; it is headquarters to the U.S. Sugar Corporation.
  a) Sweet Town
  b) Clewiston
  c) Milton

(Answer: b)

TASTE OF FLORIDA

Florida Dept. of Commerce

Fishing boats at Fernandina Beach

Something Fishy

It's impossible to indulge your taste buds in Florida without encountering sea creatures. Whether you take your food on the shell or the scale, it seems as if there's endless variety to choose from. For that, give credit where credit is due: saltwater edges three sides of the peninsula. Great grouper, minuscule grunt, pompano, yellowfin tuna, shrimp, conch, crab, sweet spiny lobster—the seafood spectrum almost demands a book instead of a menu. And the Panhandle's Apalachicola oysters (on the half-shell or fully dressed) are famous worldwide and available almost year-round.

If you're on a low-salt diet, bless Florida's 10,000 lakes and 166 rivers for their freshwater bounty. Batter-fried catfish and steamed jumbo crawfish (also known as Florida lobster) are inland favorites.

When your taste buds demand something completely out of the ordinary, alligator tail is legal as long as the 'gators stay off the endangered species list. But that's a scale of a different color. 🐟

Florida Eats

Variety certainly is one spice of life, and Florida's eats are nothing if not varied. Of course, that's to be expected in an area where so many cultures share the same 53,997 square miles. Greeks and Cubans have added moussaka, fried plantain, and black beans to Florida's banquet. Creole jambalaya and Minorcan pilau are on the menu, too. And so are Native American fry bread and mashed cassava, unusual American standards.

Traditional southern fare—fried chicken, grits, and hushpuppies—is always in vogue in central and northern parts of the state. On the nuevo or nouvelle side, unusual fruits and vegetables combined with paper-thin portions of lamb, seafood, or beef can earn a chef his or her reputation. Spicy key lime salsa, hot habanero pasta, plantain smothered in mango butter—if some menus read like romance novels that's because Florida takes its reputation as "paradise" very seriously, even where the stomach is concerned.

Comfort food is also readily available in the Sunshine State. Steak—barbecued, grilled, or fried—comes with mounds of mashed potatoes and ladles of gravy at roadside cafes and diners. Floridians do boast about their beef, and why not? After all, there are more than 20,000 ranches in the state.

Fin Festival Trivia

☛ In the mood for seafood? **November Florida Seafood Festival**, held in Apalachicola, is a festive event, and the town's riverfront atmosphere is conducive to your gastronomic pleasure. Oyster eating and shucking contests are part of the fun. *FYI:* 904-653-8051.

☛ Ah, the sweet smell of seafood gumbo and chowder, batter-fried flounder, deviled crabs, and deep-fried shrimp. For a decade, folks at the **Port Canaveral Seafood Festival** have dished out fun and food in March. Children's events are part of the celebration, too. *FYI:* Cocoa Beach area Chamber of Commerce; 407-459-2200.

The conch is Florida's official state shell

Home Cookin'

Even when you're not at home, you can satisfy your craving for home cooking. The following recipes are included not only because they are now traditional Florida fare, but because they're easy as well.

Key West Conch Salad
1 pound conch
juice of 6 Key limes or 2 Persian limes
1/2 red onion
1 cucumber, peeled, seeded, and finely chopped
1/2 cup fresh cilantro (coriander leaves)
1/2 red bell pepper, finely chopped
1 cup olive oil
1 level teaspoon leaf oregano
1 level teaspoon sugar
1/2 level teaspoon salt
1/2 level teaspoon ground black pepper
leafy lettuce

Pound the conch and chop into 1/8-inch pieces. Cover with lime juice. Cover and marinate for 24 hours. Drain. Chop onion, cucumber, cilantro, and bell pepper finely. Combine all ingredients. Refrigerate for 24 hours. Serve chilled on a bed of leafy lettuce. Serves: 4

Key Lime Mousse
4 egg whites
14-ounce can condensed milk
4 egg yolks
1 cup fresh Key lime juice or Persian lime juice
6 dark chocolate cups, 1 inch high, 3 inches wide
6 slices candied lime (available at most candy stores)

In a small bowl, beat the egg whites to firm consistency. In another bowl, mix the condensed milk and egg yolks. Add Key lime juice. With your hands, fold the egg whites into the milk mixture, using a circular motion (from bottom to top). This will form the mousse. Put into chocolate cups and decorate with candied lime slices. Serves: 6

Verona Watson's Fried Oysters

1 egg
1/2 cup water
1 dozen oysters
white cornmeal
pepper
vegetable oil for deep-frying
vinegar
lemon juice

Make an egg wash by beating the egg and water together. Dip the oysters into the egg wash and roll in white cornmeal seasoned with pepper. Chill. Deep-fry at 350 degrees for 3 to 4 minutes. Cook a little longer for real brown crispness. Serve with vinegar and lemon juice on the side for seasoning. Serves: 2.

"Key West Conch Salad," "Key Lime Mousse" and "Verona Watson's Fried Oysters" excerpted from *Tropical Cooking* © 1987 Joyce LaFray Young. Reprinted by permission of Ten Speed Press, P.O.Box 7123, Berkeley, CA 94707.

Eating Vocabulary Quiz

1) The meat dish known as vaca frita means _____ _____.
   a) flat shoe **b)** empty fruit **c)** fried cow
2) Roast pork seasoned with lots of garlic and spiced up with Key oranges is called _____.
   a) puerco rico **b)** lechon **c)** ajo!
3) Picadillo is a Cuban _____ spiced with capers and raisin sauce.
   a) casserole **b)** cake **c)** hamburger
4) Cooked conch (pronounced "konk") takes myriad forms: fritters, chowder, salad, steak. In taxonomic terms, this animal is classified as an ocean _____.
   a) fish **b)** mollusk **c)** shark

Answers: 1) c 2) b 3) c 4) b

Cuban cuisine is a main ingredient of Florida's gastronomic stew

Miami Munchies

Following the trend of most urban tourist destinations, visible Miami has been remade (and glitzed up) by outsiders for outsiders. There are pluses and minuses when it comes to food. Nouvelle Caribbean restaurants, nuevo Cubano eateries, and aficionados of native Florida cuisine multiply like gastronomic weeds. On the one hand, this may result in an unsettling stew of mispronunciation—and indigestion. On the other hand, gastronomic history—even fleeting—can be made and enjoyed here.

Mark's Place is named for premier chef Mark Militello, one of the movers and shakers when it comes to developing a native Florida cuisine. The menu is never sedentary; on the pricey side. *FYI:* 2286 N.E. 123rd St., North Miami; 305-893-6888. 🐌

Young, upwardly mobile Cuban-Americans are the inspiration for **YUCA**, where plantain-coated dolphin set off by a tamarind sauce is the norm. Don't mistake the tropical yuca—a.k.a. South American manioc or cassava—for the Southwest's yucca or agave. These are two different species, and one will not replace the other in recipes. *FYI:* 177 Giralda Ave., Coral Gables; 305-444-4448.

Allen Susser, chef-owner of **Chef Allen's** takes credit as a trail-blazer when it comes to the taste buds—for instance, lobster and crabcake with strawberry-ginger chutney or grilled tuna with asparagus mango accompanied by saffron papardelle. Think about it. *FYI:* 19088 N.E. 29th Ave., North Miami Beach; 305-935-2900.

Casa Juancho was billed the finest Spanish restaurant in the United States by *Florida Trend* magazine in 1992. Tapas, pheasant, rabbit, and Castillian-style lamb dress the menu. The wines are excellent. *FYI:* 2436 S.W. Eighth St., Miami; 305-642-2452. 🍴

You can stand in line and order up terrific Cuban sandwiches at either location of the **Latin American Cafeteria**. Prices are muy reasonable and the ambiance is squeaky clean. *FYI:* 2940 Coral Way (29th Ave.), Miami, 305-448-6809; 7950 S.W. 8th St. (79th Ave.), Miami, 305-266-9992.

Creating Cuban sandwiches in Ybor City

Florida State Archives

Florida State Archives, Fishbaugh Collection

Roadside fruit sales in Miami, 1922

Green Oranges

You don't have to visit Florida to sample Sunshine State orange juice. Every time you open a can of frozen O.J., chances are good you're boosting one of the state's top commodities. Christopher Columbus gets credit for carrying the first orange seeds to the New World. Pizarro transported them to Peru. But tales of the New World orange pale when compared to this fruit's first written mention in China around 500 B.C. One of the milestones of America's citrus history occurred following WW II. Three scientists in Florida made a surprise discovery, the result of which was commercial orange juice concentrate.

Florida oranges rate a few tips: ripe, juicy oranges may sport bright green rinds; most of the state's orange trees are growing up from lemon root stock; fruit grown closest to the ground is not as sweet as "high" fruit; oranges growing on the tree's south side are sweeter than east- or west-siders. 🍊

Yellow Limes

These days it's not easy to find real Key limes—tiny yellow fruits from the Yucatán that taste almost nothing like their green cousins. They used to grow wild in the Florida Keys, but hurricanes and development have reduced their numbers. Key limes were the original inspiration for Key lime pie.

Florida's seedless grapefruits and loose-skin tangerines are delicious, sweet, and seem to taste better when purchased at one of the state's many roadside stands.

If you want to skip citrus, you can still choose from papayas, mangoes, zapotes, guavas, avocados, strawberries, and sweet peppers (yes, they're fruits, not vegetables). 🍊

Ben Hill Griffin, Jr. (1910–1990)

One of the last of a breed of orange barons, Ben Hill Griffin, Jr., of Frostproof, spent most of his childhood hoeing, pruning, fertilizing, running sprayers, and climbing trees. He studied agriculture at the University of Florida, and his first salaried job was in a fresh-fruit packing house. Griffin went on to own his own citrus packing house in addition to a canning company. He served as president of the Florida Cattleman's Association and he was a Florida State Representative for many years.

Florida State Archives

Orange Trivia

☞ Quid pro quo: while most of Florida's oranges are growing on hardy lemon roots, California's lemons grow from orange root stock.

☞ In general, commercial citrus fruit trees are the sum of two parts: scion (one type of citrus) and rootstock (another type of citrus). Raising seedling trees takes too long for money-conscious entrepreneurs.

☞ For classic orange information, *Oranges* by John McPhee is juicy reading.

☞ Lightning kills more of Florida's orange trees than disease.

☞ Florida's orange history can be measured in freezes: 1747, 1766, 1774, 1835, 1957 and 1989 were devastating years for low temperatures.

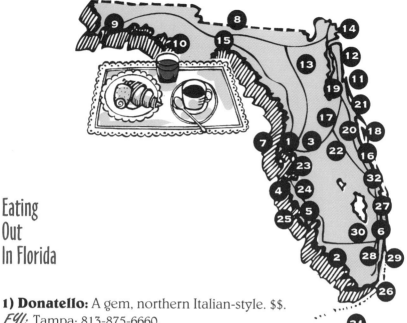

Eating
Out
In Florida

1) Donatello: A gem, northern Italian-style. $$. *FYI:* Tampa; 813-875-6660.

2) Lafite: Deluxe, American regional cuisine. $$$. *FYI:* Registry Resort Hotel, 475 Seagate Dr., Naples; 813-597-3232.

3) Mise En Place: Grilled swordfish, tournedos. $$. *FYI:* 442 W. Kennedy Blvd., Tampa; 813-254-5373.

4) Ophelia's on the Bay: Wonderful waterfront dining. $$$. *FYI:* 9105 Midnight Pass Rd., Siesta Key; 813-349-2212.

5) L'Auberge du Bon Vivant: French setting. Sweetbreads, filet mignon. $$. *FYI:* 7003 Gulf of Mexico Dr., Longboat Key; 813-383-2421.

6) Armadillo Café: Southwest picante. $$$. *FYI:* 4630 S.W. 64th Ave., Davie; 305-791-5104.

7) Tío Pepe Restaurant: Great Spanish food, sangria. $$. *FYI:* 2930 Gulf-to-Bay Blvd., Clearwater; 813-799-3082.

8) Andrew's Second Act: Steak, seafood, veal. $$$. *FYI:* 102 W. Jefferson St., Tallahassee; 904-222-2759.

9) Flounder's Chowder & Ale House: Nachos to baked oysters. $$. *FYI:* 800 Quiet Water Beach Rd., Pensacola Beach; 904-932-2003.

10) Captain Anderson's: High-volume success. $$. *FYI:* 5551 N. Lagoon Dr., Panama City Beach; 904-234-2225.

11) Saltwater Cowboy's: Seafood on stilts. $$. *FYI:* Dondanville Rd., St. Augustine; 904-471-2332.

12) Old City House: Casually elegant, seafood stew, gator fritters. $$-$$$. *FYI:* 115 Cordova St.; St. Augustine; 904-826-0781.

13) The Sovereign Restaurant: Old brick and championship cuisine. $$-$$$. *FYI:* 12 S.E. Second Ave., Gainesville; 904-378-6307.

14) 24 Miramar: Café-style, wonderful seafood, perfect pasta. $$.
FYI: 4446 Hendricks Ave., Jacksonville; 904-448-2424.
15) The Wharf: Best seafood in town. $-$$.
FYI: 4141 Apalachee Parkway, Tallahassee; 904-656-2395.
16) Bernard's Surf: Fabulous seafood, classic eatery. $$-$$$.
FYI: 2 S. Atlantic Ave., Cocoa Beach; 407-783-2401.
17) Chris's House of Beef: Landmark for beef lovers. $$.
FYI: John Young Parkway at West Colonial Dr., Orlando; 407-295-1931.
18) Dixie Crossroads: Delicious catfish, seafood. $.
FYI: 1475 Garden St., Titusville; 407-268-5000.
19) Karling's Inn: Wiener schnitzel and escargot. $$.
FYI: 4640 N. US17, DeLeon Springs; 904-985-5535.
20) Park Plaza Gardens: Veal Oscar, grilled scallops. $$-$$$.
FYI: 319 Park Ave. S., Winter Park; 407-645-2475.
21) Topaz Café and Porch: Landmark hotel, one-of-a-kind dining experience. $$-$$$.
FYI: 1224 S. Ocean Shore Blvd., Flagler Beach; 904-439-3275.
22) Vinton's New Orleans: Family business, filet mignon in blackberry sauce, Historic District. $$.
FYI: 229 E. Stuart Ave., Lake Wales; 813-676-8242.
23) Bern's Steak House: 62 different beef cuts, extensive wine list. $$.
FYI: 1208 S. Howard Ave., Tampa; 813-251-2421.
24) Carmichael's: Steamer clam roast, tenderloin of African ostrich. $$.
FYI: 1213 N. Palm Ave., Sarasota; 813-951-1771.
25) The Colony Restaurant: Beautiful setting, tarragon-seasoned rack of lamb. $$-$$$.
FYI: 1620 Gulf of Mexico Dr., Longboat Key; 813-383-5558.
26) Atlantic's Edge: Conch fritters, steamed dolphin. $$-$$$.
FYI: Cheeca Lodge, Mile Marker 82, Islamorada; 305-664-4651.
27) Café Arugula: Exceptional food, elegant café. $$$.
FYI: 3150 N. Federal Highway, Lighthouse Point; 305-785-7732.
28) Café Seville: Paella, sherry-sautéed sausage, good wine. $$.
FYI: 2768 E. Oakland Park Blvd., Fort Lauderdale; 305-565-1148.
29) Caffé Abbracchi: Designer pizzas, seafood. $$-$$$.
FYI: 318 Aragon Ave., Coral Gables; 305-441-0700.
30) La Ferme: Chicken liver mousse pâté, sautéed red snapper. $$$.
FYI: 1601 E. Sunrise Blvd., Fort Lauderdale; 305-764-0987.
31) Little Palm Island: Via the Little Torch Key launch, fine food, and palm fronds. $$$.
FYI: US1, Mile Marker 28.5, Little Torch Key
32) The Crab Pot's Old House: Oldest house in Lantana, raw bar, seafood. $-$$. *FYI:* 300 East Ocean Ave., Lantana; 407-533-5220.

Wineries

Centuries ago, wine growers discovered that nonnative grapes do not thrive in Florida's temperate to subtropical climate. In the 1930s, grape research began in earnest at Florida's universities. The result of that research was the discovery of two distinct families of wine grapes that flourish in the Sunshine State: Florida hybrid and muscadine grapes. You can sample Florida wines at the following wineries. Call ahead for hours and information.

Wineries and Breweries

1) Chataugua Vineyards: This is the largest vineyard and winery in the state. Between 400,000 and 600,000 pounds of grapes are crushed at the winery each year. Tours and tasting. *FYI:* 1330 Freeport Rd., DeFuniak Springs; 904-892-5887.

2) Lakeridge Winery & Vineyards: Distinctive wines from hybrid bunch grapes and premium table and sparkling wines from muscadine grapes. Tours and tasting. *FYI:* 19239 US27 North, Clermont; 800-476-VINE or 904-394-8627.

3) Eden Vineyards & Winery: Traditional barrel fermentation combined with modern vinification. Tram ride, nature walks, tours, and tasting. *FYI:* 19850 State Road 80, Alva; 813-728-WINE or 813-939-3550.

Breweries, Microbreweries, Pubs, and Brew Pubs

By definition, microbreweries are small and the beer is fresh. Because small breweries have a limited capacity for production and distribution, their beers may be available only at the brewery. The following list provides a taste of Florida's brew establishments. Brews are subject to change.

4) McGuire's Irish Pub: This was called the best pub in the South, maybe the nation, by *Florida Trend* magazine. McGuire and Molly keep track of it all. The menu includes McGuire's Irish Red, McGuire's Porter, McGuire's Lite, McGuire's Irish Stout, and McGuire's Root Beer, as well as Carlos McGuire's Supreme Nachos, and an Irish Wake (limit two per person). The brewing is done with the finest malted barley, Washington State hops, and yeast imported from the British Isles—no chemicals or additives. *FYI:* 600 E. Gregory St., Pensacola; 904-433-6789.

5) Kidders Brew Pub: At this microbrewery, Edison Light, Scotch Ale, Kidders' Pale Ale, Black Caesar's Porter, and Bavarian Weizen Wheat Beer are the main specialties of the house. At the moment, this is the only brewery in Southwest Florida. Brewing is completed on-site, adhering to the principles of the Bavarian Reinheitsgebot of 1516: natural ingredients only. Edward Collins, brewmaster, is a graduate of Seibel Institute of Brewing Technology, Chicago. Kidders' Scotch Ale was the winner of the Silver Medal Award at the 1992 Great American Beer Festival International Competition, Colorado. *FYI:* 11491 Cleveland Ave., Fort Myers; 813-939-BREW.

6) Sarasota Brewing Company Bar & Grill: You'll find handcrafted beers at this first microbrewery in Sarasota County. Sarasota follows the Reinheitsgebot German purity laws in the brewing process, and a long list of available (and award-winning) beers includes Sequoia Amber Lager, Midnight Pass Dark Honey Ale, Casey Key Imperial Dark Ale: Gourmet Edition, Moristan Weizen, and Boomers Oktoberfest Dark. Clinton's Presidential Pale Ale is their most expensive beer to produce. Oh, yes, there's good food, too. *FYI:* 6607 Gateway Ave., Sarasota; 813-925-BEER.

7) Hops Grill & Bar Microbrewery: You can take the tour and learn about plate frame heat exchangers and sugar extraction mash lauters. You can also sample crisp "home-brewed" beer from a frozen mug. Beers include Hops Golden (American lager style), Clearwater Light (reduced carbohydrate), and Hammerhead Red (a full-bodied, all-malt amber ale). Everything's brewed up the natural way. *FYI:* 14303 N. Dale Mabry Hwy., Tampa; 813-264-0522 or 813-871-3600.

8) Riverwalk Brewery, Inc.: This brauhaus and restaurant serves up three types of homemade German Beer—all brewed in strict accordance with German purity laws—as well as a full menu of German and American food. Lunch, dinner, brew-tour. *FYI:* 111 S.W. 2nd Ave., Ft. Lauderdale; 305-463-BEER.

THE SPORTING LIFE

Florida's amusement parks have something for almost everybody. Wet 'n Wild, a 25-acre park in Orlando, offers the brave a 70-degree angled shoot and a 115-foot-long water runway

Perfect Fit

A mong the fifty states, Florida ranks at the top as a recreational mecca. And in Florida, water tops everything. Whether your athletic preference runs to snorkeling, canoeing, kayaking, fishing, scuba diving, water-skiing, or just basking as a "beach potato," indulge yourself.

Those who prefer their leisure dry will not be disappointed. Hiking, biking, horseback riding, ballooning, bird-watching, camping—it's your call. And finally, for those who prefer to sit back—and relax—rodeos, car racing, horseracing, spring training, or jai alai may fill your spectating bill. 🐚

On Water

Some areas of Florida can be reached only by boat. That shouldn't stop you; if you don't own a water craft, you can rent one. There are more than 950 miles of state canoe trails to choose from. Maps and guides to the **Florida Recreational Trails System** are free for the asking from the Florida Department of Natural Resources. Ask for *Canoe Trails, Canoe Information Resources Guide,* and *Canoe Liveries and Outfitters Directory.* *FYI:* Div. of Recreation and Parks, Marjory Stoneman Douglas Building, 3900 Commonwealth Blvd., Tallahassee, FL 32399-3000; 904-487-4784.

Safety and boating regulations for all craft may be obtained from the **Florida Marine Patrol, Boating Safety Program**, 3900 Commonwealth Blvd., Tallahassee, FL 32399; 904-487-3671.

Boaters alert: Florida's manatees are endangered animals primarily because they cannot swim fast enough to escape careless boaters. Observe all manatee regulatory zones and caution areas—manatees have the right of way. *FYI:* Report any instance of manatee harassment, injury, or death to the Manatee Hotline; 800-DIAL-FMP.

In Water

Florida provides exceptional opportunities for freshwater and saltwater skin and scuba diving. For best visibility and warmest water, May through September are the preferred months for skin diving along the coast. The exception: conditions in the Florida Keys are excellent year-round.

For inland diving, winter is the most popular season. The cold weather controls algae, and a lower water table means a lack of precipitation, so the water is often much clearer than during the summer season.

Multi-person Recompression Chamber Sites

Naval Ship Research and
  Development Lab, Panama City
Naval Space Medical Testing,
  Pensacola
University of Miami (School of
  Marine Sciences)
Shands Teaching Hospital,
  University of Florida, Gainesville
Bay Memorial Hospital, Panama
  City

Watch out for shelling mania! It starts out with one innocent shell clutched in your hot little hand. All of a sudden, a world opens up in front of your feet—whelks, cockles, conches—and you can't make any progress without a permanent stoop. Some call it the "Sanibel Stoop" or the "Captiva Crook" because these islands are such prime shelling locations. The **Sanibel Shell Fair** (early March) attracts participants from all over the world. Don't forget the shell limit— only two per shell species per collector. If you'd rather not stoop, stop by **Neptune's Treasures** and **Showcase Shells** on Sanibel. Both shops are owned by shell experts happy to share their knowledge.

Beaches

Life's a Beach

Thank the Army Corps of Engineers as you sift the sand of Miami Beach through your toes. In the late 1970s, a $60-million sand-replacement project dumped almost 14 million cubic yards of sand here. But if beachcombing is your passion, don't limit yourself to Miami Beach. Florida provides opportunities galore to enjoy sun and surf.

1) Perdido Key State Recreation Area: A world-class beach with picnic areas and rest rooms.

2) Grayton Beach State Recreation Area: Broad sandy beach, dunes, and turquoise water. Camp, swim, surf, fish.

3) St. Andrews State Recreation Area: Main beach as well as primitive section on Shell Island. Camping and swimming.

4) T. H. Stone Memorial St. Joseph Peninsula State Park: Great shelling, sandy beaches, salt marshes.

5) St. Vincent National Wildlife Refuge: Primitive beaches accessible only by boat.

6) Dr. Julian G. Bruce St. George Island State Park: Miles and miles of beach on St. George Island bordered by Gulf of Mexico and Apalachicola Bay.

7) Anclote Key State Preserve: This barrier island has beach, a lighthouse, and incredible wildlife. Accessible by boat.

8) Treasure Island Beach: Pirates used to hide out here; now it's a popular recreational spot.

9) Greer Island: Travel north on Longboat Key to this remote peninsula which has wide beaches and grand shelling.

10) Siesta Key: This barrier island is the home of investigator Travis McGee's creator, John D. McDonald; it's also home to other writers and artists.

11) Gasparilla Island State Recreation Area: Picnic, swim, fish, shell.

12) Captiva Island: Shelling beaches extraordinaire.

13) Delnor-Wiggens Pass State Recreation Area: Fishing, swimming, boating in the gulf.

14) Tigertail Beach: Children's playground, restaurant, great family beach.

15) Fort Zachary Taylor State Historic Site: Lovely.

16) Long Key State Recreation Area: Atlantic-side multipurpose beach.

17) Cape Florida State Recreation Area: Fine, white sand at the south end of Key Biscayne. The Keys aren't great for beaches, but this is snorkel and dive heaven.

18) John U. Lloyd State Recreation Area: Very popular beach on the lower east coast.

19) Red Reef Park: Fees are high, but don't forget you're close to Boca Raton.

20) John D. MacArthur Beach State Park: Good barrier island beach, rare flora, lots of parking. Swim, fish, snorkel, shell.

21) Blowing Rocks Preserve: Nature was the sculptor here, and occasional plumes of saltwater head skyward. For scenic appreciation only.

22) Hobe Sound National Wildlife Refuge: One of the best sea turtle nesting areas in the nation.

23) Bathtub Reef: Swim and snorkel; good recreational area for the youngest set.

24) Cocoa Beach: Surfer beach.

25) Playalinda Beach: Undeveloped and popular.

26) New Smyrna Beach: Big-time development on the way; so far, rather untouched.

27) Daytona: Action, action.

28) Flagler Beach State Recreation Area: If you want to camp here, book ahead.

29) Guana River State Park: Shells, surf, and sand.

30) Jacksonville (JAX) Beach: It's crowded and popular.

31) Little Talbot Island: Beachcomber's heaven.

32) Amelia Island State Recreation Area: 200 acres of beach. 🐚

Florida State Archives

Bathing hour on Daytona Beach at Seabreeze c. 1904

Florida Dept. of Commerce

Sailing and windsurfing are favorite activities in Tampa Bay and Hillsborough Bay

Air Sports

High in Florida's sky you may spy a crimson-winged roseate spoonbill, a sleek glider, a hot air balloon, or a brightly colored parasail. Recreational opportunities don't stop at sea level or even eye level. 🐚

For the Birds

J. N. "Ding" Darling National Wildlife Refuge—5,030 acres at Sanibel Island—is named for Jay Norwood Darling, pioneer conservationist, political cartoonist, and two-time Pulitzer Prize winner. Norwood designed the first of the Migratory Bird Hunting Stamps, commonly referred to as the "Duck Stamp" program. Proceeds are used to purchase wetlands to be used for wildlife conservation.

At Ding Darling, early mornings are best for watching. If you're very lucky, you might catch a glimpse of crimson-winged roseate spoonbills flying in formation. For your life lists, there are almost 300 known bird species here, more than 50 species of reptiles and amphibians, and at least 30 mammal species. The sparkling beaches provide excellent shelling if you know where to look. For instance, boats from Ding Darling will carry you to shoals off Cayo Costa State Preserve for shelling in winter at low tide. There is a shellers limit: two live shell specimens. Sea urchins, sand dollars, and sea stars are protected, and there is a stiff fine and possible jail sentence for those who ignore the law. A few rules apply to all of Florida's wildlife areas: don't feed the animals; don't harm wildlife; drive slowly to avoid hitting animals. 🐚

Paynes Prairie State Preserve is wet marshland; birds are abundant. FYI: Micanopy; 904-466-3397.

Myakka River State Park—one of the oldest in the state—has a winter bird-watching program designed just for beginners. *FYI:* east of Sarasota.

The **Madalyn Baldwin Center for Birds of Prey**, run by the Florida Audubon Society, is designed to rehabilitate injured raptors (hawks, owls, eagles, falcons, ospreys, and vultures). *FYI:* Maitland; 407-645-3826.

Corkscrew Swamp Sanctuary, a wilderness refuge, shelters a variety of birds, including wood storks. *FYI:* Immokalee; 813-657-3771.

From the ground looking up: some of Florida's most graceful birds

Tee Off

Golf is a $5 billion industry in Florida. The state is equipped with premier courses, and several national golf events take place here each year. The **Pensacola Open Golf Tourney** is played in Pensacola each October, Tampa is the site of the **GTE World Cup Challenge** in November, and the **South Seas Golf Tournament** takes place on Captiva Island in December. During July, the **Southern Amateur Golf Tournament** is an annual event in Orlando. *FYI:* For the official "Florida Golf Guide," contact the Florida Sports Foundation; 904-488-8347.

The Florida Trail

Happy Trails

Pinellas Trail: More than 16 miles of paved trail. c/o Pinellas County Park Department, 631 Chestnut St., Clearwater, FL 34616; 813-581-2953.

Tallahassee-St. Mark's Historic Railroad State Trail: This was Florida's first designated state trail, and it follows the abandoned Tallahassee-St. Mark's railbed. Bicycling, jogging, walking, skating, and horseback riding are all allowed. Sixteen miles of paved trail stretching from Tallahassee to the coast. *FYI:* 1022 DeSoto Park Dr., Tallahassee, FL 32301; 904-922-6007.

Gainesville-Hawthorne State Trail: This 16-mile gravel surface trail is designated for walking, cycling, and horseback riding. *FYI:* c/o Paynes Prairie State Preserve, Route 2, Box 41, Micanopy, FL 32667; 904-466-3397.

Withlacoochee State Trail: A new 47-mile rail trail from Dunellon to Trilby. *FYI:* c/o Ft. Cooper State Park, 3100 Old Floral City Rd., Inverness, FL 32650; 904-394-2280.

Green Swamp State Trail: Twenty-seven-mile rail trail from Polk City north to SR50. *FYI:* c/o Lake Louisa State Park, 12569 State Park Dr., Clermont, FL 32711; 904-394-2280.

Florida Trail: This dirt hiking trail—being developed by the Florida

Trail Association—already stretches more than 1,000 miles through Florida. Ultimately, it will connect Big Cypress National Preserve with Blackwater State Forest. Cycling is prohibited in most places. *FYI:* P.O. Box 13708, Gainesville, FL 32604; 904-378-8823. 🐾

Florida State Archives

Go Fish

Florida licenses are required for both fresh and saltwater fishing. Before you cast, keep in mind that a line of demarcation between salt and freshwater has been designated in streams, rivers, and bayous of coastal areas. When saltwater fishing, certain species are encountered in different areas.

☛ Northeast Atlantic Coast surf casting: blues, redfish, and drum
☛ Central East Coast inshore and in the surf: trout, redfish, drum, tripletail, Jack Crevalle
☛ Lower East Coast Gulf Stream: marlin, mako shark, tuna, sailfish
☛ The Keys: trout, snapper, bonefish, tarpon, grouper, barracuda, wahoo
☛ Northwest Gulf Coast: blue runner, grouper, flounder, red snapper
☛ Upper Gulf Coast: redfish, grouper, tarpon (in summer), flounder
☛ Middle Gulf Coast: tarpon, grouper, snook, kingfish, mackerel
☛ Lower Gulf Coast: pompano, snook, redfish

Florida black bass are the world's largest. Largemouth bass, smallmouth bass, spotted bass, and Suwannee bass are the four recognized varieties. The **Bass Angler's Top 100 Tournament** is held in Clewiston each December. ⋟

Black bass caught in the St. John's River in the late 1940s.

Florida State Archives

Birds in Distress

I f you come across a hooked or tangled seabird when shore fishing, the victim should be gathered in a shirt, towel, or blanket, and the hook removed. Never leave monofilament line attached to a bird; the animal will almost certainly drown. If possible, take any injured bird to a bird sanctuary for further care.

Florida Dept. of Commerce

Jai alai can make folks do off-the-wall things

Balls!

What is one of the oldest ball games in the world? And what is known as the fastest—the ball often moves at 150 mph— on two feet? If you guessed jai alai, you're in the know; the sport is a puzzle to most folks. Out of only 11 places in the United States where the game is played, 10 are in Florida. Frontons, cavernous indoor courts, dot the Gold Coast.

This sport dates back to the fifteenth century and the Pyrenees, where an innovative Basque decided to use a bread basket to heave and catch the ball. The basket is the *cesta*, and the ball is the *pelota*. Singles and doubles matches are played out in the three-walled *concha* (court) where players (*pelotaris*) try to outfinesse each other. Usually 14 games lasting about 15 minutes each, are played. Your action is placing bets: win, place, show, daily doubles, superfectas, trifectas—you name it. 🐚

Grapefruit League

Grapefruit League season is spring training: the time baseball's pros come to Florida to shape up. More than a million fans attend games, and millions of dollars are pumped into local economies.

Spring Training

1) Osceola County Stadium and Sports Complex: Houston Astros warm up here; Kissimmee; 407-933-5400.

2) Cincinnati Reds Spring Training Complex: You got it, the Reds; Plant City; 813-752-1878.

3) Lee County Sports Complex: This $15 million facility was built especially for the Minnesota Twins; Fort Myers; 813-335-2342.

4) Baseball Stadium City: 7,000-seat complex for the Kansas City Royals; Haines City; 813-424-7130.

5) Homestead Stadium: A $20 million complex for the Cleveland Indians; Homestead; 305-358-5885.

6) Fort Lauderdale Stadium: This is New York Yankee country; Fort Lauderdale; 305-776-1921.

7) West Palm Beach Municipal Stadium: The Atlanta Braves and the Montreal Expos share this one; West Palm Beach; Braves: 407-683-6100; Expos: 407-684-6801.

8) Port St. Lucie County Sports Complex: Warm-up time for the New York Mets; Port St. Lucie; 407-871-2100.

9) Holman Stadium: Seventh Inning Stretch, Los Angeles Dodgers; Vero Beach; 407-569-4900.

10) Cocoa Expo: It's spring fever for the Florida Marlins; Cocoa; 407-639-3976.

11) Charlotte County Stadium: Texas Rangers do it here; Port Charlotte; 813-625-9500.

12) Al Lang Stadium: The St. Louis Cardinals make a pitch; St. Petersburg; 813-822-3384.

13) Ed Smith Stadium: Chicago White Sox country; Sarasota; 813-954-4101.

14) Jack Russell Stadium: Philadelphia Phillies; Clearwater; 813-441-8638.

15) McKechnie Field: Pittsburgh Pirates; Bradenton; 813-747-3031.

Florida Dept. of Commerce

South Florida is polo country, and the Polo Challenge Cup is held each January in West Palm Beach

Good Breeding

Breeder Carl Rose can be thanked for Florida's thoroughbred industry. In 1917 Rose recognized the state's natural attributes for what they were—the ingredients of prime breeding land. In the 1930s he established Rosemere, his 500-acre farm.

In 1956, a colt named Needles became the state's first Kentucky Derby and Belmont Stakes champion. Today, Florida boasts the nation's third largest thoroughbred industry. Ocala is famous for its stud farms. ❧

Sport Trivia Quiz

1) Jai alai, an ancient Basque game, is pronounced _____.
  a) jay alay **b)** high lie **c)** eet eleet
2) Jai alai means _____.
  a) merry festival **b)** jump around **c)** high flyer
3) Daytona International Speedway is where the world's fastest _____ race.
  a) thoroughbreds **b)** rockets **c)** autos
4) Beach auto races were held in the _____ when manufacturers vied for new records.
  a) 1820s and 1830s **b)** morning **c)** 1930s and 1940s

Answers: 1) b 2) a 3) c 4) c

Rodeo Fever

At least ten months of the year, Florida is rodeo land at the heart of the nation's professional rodeo circuit. Arcadia boasts the state's largest purse for professional competition: $18,000. The city of Davie has a dozen rodeos per year. Statewide, there are more than 25 pro rodeos to be seen during the year. Local amateur competitions are too numerous to count, but contact the chamber of commerce in the area you plan to visit for information. For a complete listing (see partial listing below) of PRCA rodeos and events, call 719-593-8840.

January
  Fort Myers
  Davie
February
  Hollywood
  Tampa
  Brighton
March
  Arcadia
  Okeechobee
  Naples
April
  Odessa

May
  Miami
June
  Marianna
July
  Arcadia
August
  Davie
September
  Ocala
October
  Davie

Football

The **Miami Dolphins** and the **Tampa Bay Buccaneers** are Florida's two professional football teams. An additional half-dozen college football teams fill the season's roster. The Orange Bowl, the Citrus Bowl, the Gator Bowl, and the Hall of Game Bowl are just some of the football games to be seen in Florida's major stadiums in Tallahassee, Orlando, Gainesville, Jacksonville, Miami, and Tampa. The largest stadium, the Gator Bowl in Jacksonville, seats 81,000 sports fans.

Florida Dept. of Commerce

STATE OF THE ARTS

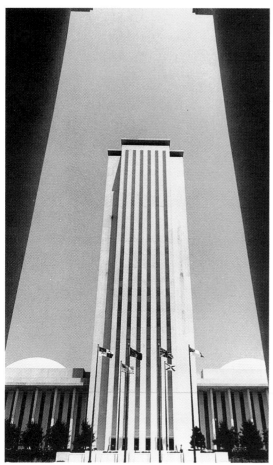

State capitol, Tallahasee

For Art's Sake

If you thought Florida was just beaches, sunshine, and hurricanes, think again. The state is home to symphony orchestral groups, performance artists, major art galleries, and museums. To honor some of the people who have contributed to the state's arts, the **Florida Artist Hall of Fame** was created by Florida's 1986 Legislature. Explore the Hall of Fame on the Plaza level of the Capitol in Tallahassee.

1) Appleton Museum of Art/Cultural Center: European, African, and Asian fine arts. *FYI:* Ocala; 904-236-5050.

2) Art and Culture Center of Hollywood: Contemporary art. *FYI:* Hollywood, 305-921-3274.

3) Art Museum at Florida International University: European and North and South American drawings and paintings. *FYI:* Miami; 305-348-2890.

4) Cummer Gallery of Art: Paintings by the masters, Asian collection, Meissen porcelain. *FYI:* Jacksonville; 904-355-0630.

5) DeLand Museum of Art: 19th- and 20th-century American fine arts and pre-Columbian art. *FYI:* DeLand; 904-734-4371.

6) Florida State University Fine Arts Gallery and Museum:
European, Asian, and Peruvian art. *FYI:* Tallahassee; 904-644-6836.
7) George D. and Harriet W. Cornell Fine Arts Center:
Renaissance and 19th- and 20th-century American art. *FYI:* Winter
Park; 407-646-2526.
8) Hibel Museum of Art: Porcelains, doll collection. *FYI:* Palm
Beach; 407-833-6870.
9) John and Mabel Ringling Museum of Art: Houses the world's
most important collection of works by Flemish painter Pierre Paul
Rubens. There is also a Circus Gallery complete with calliopes and
memorabilia, and the **Asolo Theatre**, which originally stood in Italy.
FYI: Sarasota; 813-355-5101.
10) Lightner Museum: Tiffany glass, 19th-century decorative arts,
Indian artifacts. *FYI:* St. Augustine; 904-824-2874.
11) Lowe Art Museum: Renaissance, baroque, and rococo art.
FYI: Coral Gables; 305-284-3535.
12) Museum of Art: Photography and 20th-century paintings.
FYI: Boca Raton; 407-392-2500.
13) Museum of Art: Paintings and sculpture. *FYI:* Fort Lauderdale;
305-763-6464.
14) Museum of Arts and Sciences: Fossils, Tumucuan Indian mate-
rial, Florida collection. *FYI:* Daytona Beach; 904-255-0285.
15) Norton Gallery and School of Art: Chinese jades, American
and French paintings. *FYI:* West Palm Beach; 407-832-5194.
16) Orlando Museum of Art: African and pre-Columbian art.
FYI: Orlando; 407-896-4231.

Museums
and
Art Centers

Florida Dept. of Commerce

Ringling Museum, Sarasota

17) Pensacola Museum of Art: American fine art. *FYI:* Pensacola; 904-432-6247.

18) Polk Museum of Art: 15th- through 19th-century European ceramics. *FYI:* Lakeland; 813-688-7743.

19) Dali Museum: Opened in 1982, the museum contains the world's largest collection of works by the Spanish surrealist Salvador Dali. There are more than 90 oils, 200 watercolors and drawings, and 1,000 prints. *FYI:* St. Petersburg; 813-823-3767.

20) Tampa Museum of Art: Greek and Roman artifacts, fine art. *FYI:* Tampa; 813-223-8130.

21) University of Florida Gallery: Photography, Native American fine arts. *FYI:* Gainesville; 904-392-0201.

22) University of South Florida Art Galleries: Contemporary, folk, and ethnic art. *FYI:* Tampa; 813-974-2849.

23) Viscaya: John Deering's Italian Renaissance villa is adorned with exquisite European antiques, paintings, sculpture, and oriental carpets. Ten acres of formal gardens grace the grounds. *FYI:* Miami; 305-579-2813. ⁊

Florida Dept. of Commerce

Van Wetzel Pavilion, Sarasota

Performance Art and Art in Public

Live, in living color, mistakes and all, there's nothing quite like performance art or public performers. Florida has been home to many performing artists, some of them world-famous.

Greater Miami Convention and Visitors Bureau

Vizcaya

In 1914, farm magnate John Deering hired 1,000 workers to create his $15 million estate: an Italian Renaissance villa complete with ten acres of formal gardens. Interior decorator Paul Chalfin used Vizcaya to launch his career. Architect F. Burrall Hoffman, Jr. was commissioned to design the house to hold the exquisite art collection. The architecture is spectacular, and, outside, the botanical gardens overlook the sculptured Stone Barge anchored in Biscayne Bay. The barge was designed by landscape architect Diego Suarez. *FYI:* Miami; 305-579-2813.

Musical River

Composer Stephen Foster probably never laid eyes on the Suwannee River; he was residing in Pittsburgh when he labored over a song about a river down south. (His first choice was South Carolina's Peedee River, but try rhyming that one.) His "Old Folks at Home" has since become a classic—and the official state song. The **Stephen Foster State Folk Culture Center** pays homage to the composer. It is also where the Department of State's **Florida Folklife Program** organizes events during the year such as the Old-Fashioned Fourth of July Celebration and the Florida Folk Festival, which is held on Memorial Day weekend. *FYI:* White Springs, off US41 North; 904-397-2733.

Ray Charles (b. 1930)

Ray Charles began life in the small town of Greenville close to the Georgia border. As a boy, he was blinded when he tried to save his younger brother from drowning. Charles studied piano at the Florida School for the Deaf and Blind in St. Augustine. His soulful style continues to influence young musicians.

Florida State Archives

A Year in the Life of Public Art

January: Florida Keys Renaissance Fair. *FYI:* Marathon; 305-743-5417.
February: Miami Film Festival. *FYI:* Miami; 305-377-3456.
March: Bluegrass Festival. *FYI:* Kissimmee; 407-847-5000.
April: Shakespeare Festival. *FYI:* Orlando; 407-363-5871.
May: Sunfest. *FYI:* West Palm Beach; 407-659-5980.
June: Friday Extra Concerts, Lowry Park. *FYI:* Tampa; 813-223-1111.
July: Miccosukee Crafts and Music Festival. *FYI:* Miami
August: Boca Festival Days. *FYI:* Boca Raton; 407-395-4443.
September: Tampa Bay Performing Arts Center. *FYI:* Tampa; 813-221-1045.
October: National Jazz Festival. *FYI:* Jacksonville; 904-366-6600.
November: Great Gulf Coast Arts Festival. *FYI:* Penscola; 904-434-1234 or out of state, 800-874-1234.
December: Florida Tournament of Bands. *FYI:* St. Petersburg; 813-898-6354.

Florida State Archives

Jimmy Buffet (left) and Gov. Graham during the 1984 Press Corps Skits

Musical Trivia

☛ **Jimmy Buffet began his career playing in Florida bars. His albums include** *Havana Daydreamin'* **and** *Coconut Telegraph.* **Buffet now lives in Florida and Colorado.**
☛ **The late musical group Lynyrd Skynyrd—creators of the albums** *Bullets* **and** *Nuthin' Fancy*—**hailed from Florida.**
☛ **Floridian Frederick Delius composed the "Florida Suite" and "Dance Rhapsody #2."**
☛ **Stephen Foster was the author of "Oh! Susanna" and "My Old Kentucky Home."**

Literary Florida

Florida's land—its swamps, flatlands, seashores, and rolling hills—marks the spirit of its people; almost as noticeably, landscape guides the shape the word takes on the page. Some of the most memorable writers use setting—an indelible sense of place—as character. Their land- and cityscapes are as unforgettable as any character. Florida has had its share of literary lions, and they've been chronicling the state for centuries. Perhaps anyone who was bullheaded enough to put up with yellow fever and pirates wanted to make darn sure that future generations would read all about it. ༄

Zora Neale Hurston (1891-1960)

Born in Eatonville in 1891, Zora Neale Hurston grew up to become one of Florida's leading authors. She was educated at Howard University, Barnard College, and Columbia University and became an anthropologist in addition to publishing novels, essays, and short stories. *Their Eyes Were Watching God* (1936) tells the story of the 1928 hurricane's effect on poor Florida farmers. It is also cited as the first black feminist novel of the twentieth century. A writer of the Harlem Renaissance, Hurston was criticized for her decision to celebrate black folk culture in literature instead of directly protesting racial oppression. Although her work was overlooked for years, Hurston is now celebrated for her literary genius. Her works include *Tell My Horse* (1938), *Dust Tracks on a Road* (1942), and *Seraph on the Suwanee* (1948).

Florida State Archives

Ernest Miller Hemingway (1899-1961)

Hemingway was born in Oak Park, Illinois in 1899, and came of age as the world was going to war. After working as a reporter for the Kansas City *Star*, he enlisted in Italy's army to serve as ambulance driver and infantryman. His Key West association began in 1928 on the advice of novelist John Dos Passos. When Hemingway wasn't writing in Florida, he hung out with the "Key West Mob"—charterboat captain Eddie "Bra" Saunders and Joe "Josie" Russell, another captain who survived in part by running rum from Havana to Key West.

Florida State Archives

During the Spanish Civil War and WWII, Hemingway served as a correspondent. He received the Nobel Prize for literature in 1954. His books include *The Old Man and the Sea, A Farewell to Arms, To Have and Have Not,* and *A Moveable Feast. FYI:* A Hemingway Collection is located at the Monroe County Library; **The Hemingway House** is located at 907 Whitehead St., Key West.

Florida Dept. of Commerce

"Hemingway's Favorite Bar"—Sloppy Joe's—has relocated several times since Hemingway first encountered Joe "Josie" Russell at his bar, a shack situated near the Key West naval base. When Hemingway left for Cuba, a collection of the writer's papers, manuscripts, and letters were locked away in Sloppy Joe's "hole." After Josie Russell's death in 1941, Hemingway rarely returned to Key West. Today, you can ponder the fleeting nature of fame as you gaze at two of Hemingway's uncashed royalty checks that hang in the bar. *FYI:* 201 Duval St., Key West.

Literary Florida

Marjorie Kinnan Rawlings (1896-1953)

Florida State Archives

Born in Washington, D.C., Rawlings had a career as a journalist before settling in Cross Creek in 1928. Florida's environment, people, and folklore flavor her stories and novels, which include *The Yearling* (1933), *Golden Apples* (1935), and *Cross Creek* (1942).

Florida Literary Quiz

1) What Florida key plays an important role in Thomas McGuane's 1973 novel, *Ninety-two in the Shade*?

2) What 1942 novel by Robert Wilder was later the basis for a television soap opera?

3) Who set many of his most famous plays in the south, close to his real home in Key West?

4) What 1942 book by author Marjorie Kinnan Rawlings was the subject of lawsuits by Floridians?

5) John D. MacDonald was the author of the well-known Travis McGee series. In 1977, he also published a novel about the hurricane destruction of a condominium on a fictional Florida key. What is the book's title?

6) Singer/songwriter Jimmy Buffet has turned successful author; his latest book is *Where Is Joe Merchant*? What was the title of his first book?

7) What literary event is held in Key West each January?

Answers:
1) Key West 2) *Flamingo Road* 3) Tennessee Williams 4) *Cross Creek* 5) *Condominium* 6) *Tales from Margaritaville* 7) Key West Writers' Workshop

Who Said It?

☞ "The Amazing Kingdom of Thrills reopened with only a minimal drop in attendance, thanks to a three-for-one ticket promotion that included a ride on Dickie the Dolphin, whose amorous behavior was now inhibited by four trainees armed with electric stun guns."

—Carl Hiaasen, *Native Tongue*

☞ "Ships at a distance have every man's wish on board. For some they come in with the tide. For others they sail forever on the horizon, never out of sight, never landing until the Watcher turns his eyes away in resignation, his dreams mocked to death by Time. That is the life of men."

—Zora Neal Hurston, *Their Eyes Were Watching God*

☞ "The sun was in Robert Jordan's eyes and the bridge showed only in outline. Then the sun lessened and was gone and looking up through the trees at the brown, rounded height that it had gone behind, he saw, now, that he no longer looked into the glare, that the mountain slope was a delicate new green and that there were patches of old snow under the crest."

—Ernest Hemingway, *For Whom the Bell Tolls*

☞ "A chill came over Jody. Buck was worse than his mother to take away pleasure. He lingered a moment with the fawn, stroking it. It moved its sleepy head and nuzzled his fingers. Buck could not know of the closeness. It was all the better for being secret. He left the fawn and went to the basin and washed, too. The touch of the fawn had left his hands scented with a faint grassy pungency. He hated to wash it away, but decided that his mother might not find it as pleasant."

—Marjorie Kinnan Rawlings, *The Yearling*

☞ "Walking over to Ocean Drive was no problem. The evening was balmy, and television had even made the streets safer. If you and a sinister stranger are the only people on a dark street, you might be in trouble. But when you are part of a crowd headed for a trendy South Beach club or restaurant, there is safety in numbers."

—Edna Buchanan, *Contents Under Pressure*

Film Florida

Lights, Camera, Action!

The film industry means money wherever the action is, in this case, Florida. Since 1900, scads of movies have been filmed—at least in part—in the Sunshine State. In the 1940s, Tarzan (as performed by Johnny Weismuller), Jane (Maureen O'Sullivan, of course), and Cheetah arrived at Silver Springs for the filming of six jungle movies. Those vines that the big guy swung on were actually ropes dangling over the springs.

The Florida town known as Rock Harbor is a famous example of the power of the film industry to create life in its own image. Never heard of Rock Harbor? There's a good reason. Promoters and developers thought it was a great idea to piggyback their town on the publicity given Bogart and Bacall's 1948 drama, *Key Largo*. Enough signatures were collected on a local petition to ratify a name change. Postal authorities approved the "stage name" in 1952, and Rock Harbor officially became Key Largo. Yes, a few scenes of the movie were shot in the Caribbean Club bar; the rest of Key Largo was filmed on a sound stage in Hollywood. The next time you're a couch potato and watching old movies, notice the fog and kelp. Director John Huston knew how to create great drama, but he didn't know the Keys, which are devoid of both fog and kelp.

In the tradition of make-your-own tradition, the owner of Key Largo's Holiday Inn purchased the actual riverboat Bogart navigated in the movie *African Queen* (filmed mostly in England). You can actually take a cruise on the African Queen for a fee. What does all this have to do with Hollywood and the film business? It's all about make believe.

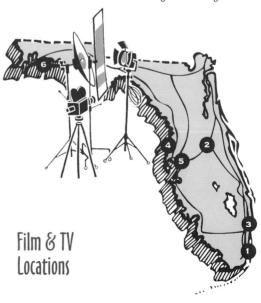

Film & TV
Locations

Film & TV Locations

1) Miami:
Key West (TV), 1993
The Bodyguard, 1992
Miami Blues, 1988
Miami Vice (TV), 1984-1987
Splash, 1983
Airport 77, 1976

2) Orlando:
Passenger 57, 1992
Lethal Weapon 3, 1992

3) Fort Lauderdale:
Revenge of the Nerds, 1987
Where the Boys Are Now, 1983
Caddy Shack, 1979

4) Clearwater:
Cocoon, 1984

5) Tampa:
Cop and 1/2, 1992

6) Fort Walton Beach:
Jaws 2, 1977

Florida State Archives

Johnny Weismuller, star of Tarzan films, on location at Florida's Silver Springs c. 1950

Film Festivals

Miami Film Festival—
February

Greater Fort
Lauderdale Film
Society Festival and
Market—November
Attracts major film
stars, directors, and
producers. The GLF
Film Society also
hosts regular screen-
ings througout year.
FYI: 2374 N. Federal
Hwy; 305-764-4900.

BUILDING FLORIDA

Architectural Time

1800s: In north Florida, practical colonial frame houses evolved into much grander columned mansions a la Southern planters. The column was the ultimate symbol of status for plantation society, as it was for early Greeks and Romans. In south Florida's Keys, salvage barons acquired fortunes and applied ship-building skills to eclectic Conch style homes which were a combination of Bahamian, Creole, and New England frame style. Prosperity brought the frills: verandas, gingerbread, and gables.

Gilded Age: At the turn of the century, railroads, petroleum, liquor, shipping, and automobiles were creating American millionaires. Men like James Deering, Henry Morrison Flagler, and Henry Plant created luxury and splendor in the wilderness. The first two decades of the twentieth century were a time of palatial homes, grand hotels, private railcars, and no income tax.

1920–1925: During the Florida Land Boom, the state's population grew at a rate four times that of any other. Influenced by frame Cracker houses, builders touted the "bungalow" as the new single-family dwelling. At the same time, subdivisions grew up around themes—a Mediterranean village, a land of Arabian nights, or a Southwest Pueblo-style village.

1930s: World War II drove European artists and architects to America; they brought Art Deco with them. This was a truly modern

Florida State Archives

During the Florida Land Boom, these mangrove trees fell victim to developer George E. Merrick (second from left) and his Tahiti Beach recreation area

The sleek skyline of Greater Miami

style—Miami Beach went wild with tropical and nautical motifs—and the public loved it.

International Style: New technologies supplied new architectural inspiration. Variations on the theme included clean lines, no ornamentation, glass, stone, "anything goes."

Modernism: The aim here is pure form. 🐚

Carl Graham Fisher was a newspaperman; he was also a master of the advertising campaign. Fisher never went beyond elementary school, but that didn't stop him from becoming a millionaire five times over before he was forty. It was Fisher who created Miami Beach by cutting down mangroves, dredging on a massive scale, and filling. His embellishments included tennis courts, polo fields, golf courses, and grandstands. Fisher's five hotels—the Flamingo, Lincoln, Nautilus, King Cole, and Boulevard—attracted the glitz-and-glitter set. The Florida Bust and the crash of 1929 left Fisher broke; he died in debt.

Frank Lloyd Wright designed a chapel and six other buildings on the campus of Florida Southern College. Steel, glass, and sand are the elements the architect felt best represented Florida and his own architectural vision. Although interior and landscape alterations have occurred, this is one of the few places in the world where you can see multiple Wright buildings. On weekdays, pick up a campus map at the administration building. *FYI:* Ingraham Ave., Lakeland; 813-680-4111.

Miami Beach Art Deco

The 1930s in **Miami Beach** were bumper crop years, architecturally speaking, when Art Deco resort buildings sprouted and grew at the rate of about one hundred a year. The new style was innovative, cheerful, and based on geometic angles and popular flash; the aim was to attract middle-class tourists. Since then, alternating hard times and good times have left their mark on this area. Today, the **Art Deco District of Old Miami Beach**, "South Beach," is a designated local and national historic district. In the area roughly bordered by Ocean, Lenox Court, and 5th and 23rd streets, there are more than 800 historic buildings; this Deco District contains the largest concentration of Deco in the nation.

For you, the wanderer, explorer, or connossieur, this means the chance to pick out and savor the ziggurats (stepped roofs), the overhanging shades, the bas relief sculpture, the vertical planes, the color, and the whimsey that are all part of Deco. Ocean Drive (between 5th and 20th streets) is a great walk for a quick Deco fix. *FYI:* You can get a map, or take a Saturday walking tour, if you contact the Miami Design Preservation League, 661 Washington Ave., P.O. Box Bin L, Miami, FL 33119; 305-672-2014. 🐌

C'ad'Zan

Wealthy circus impresario John Ringling imported artisans from around the world to craft his 30-room mansion, **C'ad'Zan**. Mabel Ringling (John's wife) decided to have the mansion modeled after a Venetian Doges' Palace. Thomas Martin created the original design but Ringling balked at the estimate of $450,000. Architect Dwight James Baum took over—and C'ad'Zan ultimately cost more than the original bid; nevertheless, it was a masterpiece. The walls are stucco, the windows are Venetian glass, many frescoes adorn ceilings, arches and balconies are everywhere. A museum houses the world's most important collection of works by Flemish painter Pierre Paul Rubens. *FYI:* Sarasota; 813-355-5101.

Florida State Archives

The Americana is now the Sheraton Bal Harbor

Architect Morris Lapidus had complete control when he designed the **Americana Hotel**. Although Lapidus studied architecture in order to pursue a career as a set designer, he was unable to find work in the theater. He did however, find success as an architect. Expansive curves, curved walls, floating ceilings, irregular shapes, and ornamentalism were his trademarks. The hotels Fountainbleau and Eden Rock are also Lapidus creations. ✍

Addison Mizner (1872-1933)

Addison Mizner was part salesman, speculator, artist, designer, landscape expert, and interior decorator. He was not a formally trained architect. But when his plans to die in Palm Beach—he arrived in 1918, 45 years old, sick and discouraged—were thwarted by his own stamina, he instead designed the Everglades Club for sewing machine heir Paris Singer. Mizner designed more than 50 million dollars' worth of Palm Beach mansions, and made plans for his own resort city, Boca Raton. Vanderbilts, Whitneys, and Wanamakers paid in grand scale for the opulent splendor and romance of his designs. Although his architectural style was labeled a bastard style by critics, Mizner earned the praise of Frank Lloyd Wright, sculptor Jo Davidson, and designer Harvey Corbett.

Born near San Francisco, as a child Mizner traveled with his family and discovered Spanish architecture. Later, he earned his keep as a boxer, salesman, gold rusher, and hobnobber before circumstances finally brought him to Palm Beach. The great land boom eventually busted Mizner. Investors pulled their cash from the Boca Raton project, and although Mizner made good the debts, he was financially ruined. Boca Raton ultimately flourished, but the architect never recovered. *FYI:* Boca Raton Chamber of Commerce, 1800 North Route 1; 407-395-4433; the Historical Society of Palm Beach County has a collection of Mizner furniture and architectural drawings.

El Mirasol, the residence of E. T. Stotesbury, was built by Addison Mizner. Another Mizner home, Playa Rienta has been called one of the great American homes

Henry Morrison Flagler (1830-1913)

Hard work, a socially elevating marriage, and ruthless business deals brought Henry Morrison Flagler from his modest beginnings as a poor minister's son to Standard Oil Company magnate. In the late 1880s, when the government in Tallahassee offered free land to anyone who would construct a railroad, Henry Flagler and Henry Plant both responded. Flagler covered Florida's east coast with tracks all the way to Key West while Plant opened up the west coast and Central Florida. Affected boom towns became chic overnight as the Plants and the Flaglers spent millions of dollars constructing and furnishing their respective and assorted grand hotels. The Ponce de León, the Cordova, and the Alcazar were three Flagler hotels in St. Augustine.

Florida Dept. of Commerce

Henry Flagler's 55-room mansion, Whitehall (built in Palm Beach in 1901), now houses the Flagler Museum

Dream Houses

For two decades, Ed Leedskalnin mined, hauled, and carved 1,110 tons of coral to create his three-acre fantasy known as **Coral Castle**. *FYI:* near Homestead Air Force Base.

Conrad Schuck was one of a rather large group: those who come to the Sunshine State to die and then go on to live a long life. Believing he had but one good year left, Schuck left Pittsburgh and relocated his wife and nine children to Bartow, Florida. There, he broke ground in 1926 on **Wonder House**, a four-story mansion with bathing pools on porches, a cistern on the roof, a vented fireplace, and rubber flooring—all ahead of its time. There were even mirrors so one could sit in the bathtub on the third floor and see who was at the front door. *FYI:* Bartow.

Florida State Archives

Live Oak Plantation (c. 1889) was once the home of Florida Gov. John Branch. The house burned in 1894.

Florida's Plantations

When Florida became U.S. territory in 1821, the Panhandle's fertile soil offered new opportunity to cotton planters from the Old South. Southern planters had an advantage over early pioneers; these landed gentry had African slaves to clear woods and to construct roads, bridges, and buildings—to create a new world. Broad two-storied porches and columns, however rudimentary, were standard features of this plantation style.

Conch Style

Florida State Archives

Due to the salvage business, Key West was the nation's wealthiest city per capita by 1850

Thanks to pirates, treacherous weather, wild currents, and the Florida Reef, shipping off 19th-century Florida was a very risky business. Those ships that escaped Blackbeard, Gasparillo, and Black Caesar often ran aground, and shipwrecks made Key West a rich city. Once Florida became U.S. territory, Key West was the perfect location for legiti-

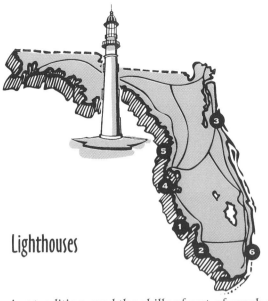

Lighthouses

mate "wreckers" as merchandise foundered on the reefs. The wrecking business stayed strong until the Civil War; 1855 was a high point with almost 3 million dollars' worth of salvage business. Key West islanders, called Conchs, developed a distinctive style of architecture based on the influence of tropical ports of call, the New England sailing tradition, and the skills of out-of-work ship's carpenters. Verandas, louvered shutters, cisterns, and widows' walks are typical of the style.

1) Port Boca Grande Lighthouse Park: This 1890s lighthouse overlooks Boca Grande Pass. 41 feet above water. *FYI:* Boca Grande.

2) Sanibel Lighthouse: 1884. Picnic, pier fish, swim, or boat here. 98 feet above water. *FYI:* Sanibel Lighthouse Park, Sanibel Island.

3) Ponce de León Lighthouse: The tallest in America, at 159 feet above water, it is open to the public. Ponce de León flashed every ten seconds from 1887 to 1970. Original equipment is on display. *FYI:* Ponce Inlet, south of Daytona Beach.

4) Egmont Key State Park: This is the only manned lighthouse in the nation. It stands on a 440-acre key that served as a detainment area for Seminoles captured during the Third Seminole War. This was also the site of a Union Navy base during the Civil War. 85 feet above water. *FYI:* mouth of Tampa Bay, accessible by private boat only; 813-893-2627.

5) Anclote Key State Preserve: This area features an 1887 federal lighthouse on the southern tip of the island; Gulf waters off a 4-mile-long beach, tall pines, and nesting ospreys, bald eagle, piping plover. You must bring your own water and supplies and take them away with you. *FYI:* 3 miles off Tarpon Springs reached only by private boat; contact Anclote Key State Preserve, c/o Caladesi Island State Park, #1 Causeway Blvd., Dunedin, FLA 34698; 813-469-5918.

6) Cape Florida Lighthouse: This lighthouse was completed in 1825 and stands on Key Biscayne. Offshore, reefs and sandbars wrecked many ships. Ranger tours are available. *FYI:* Key Biscayne; 305-361-5811.

THE SPIRIT OF FLORIDA

Florida State Archives

A Florida sink in Winter Park

Healthy Soaks

P once de León had his work cut out for him in his search for the fountain of youth among the state's 300 natural springs: at least 27 "first magnitude" springs flow out of Florida's earth at a rate of 100 cubic feet or more per second. It's still a secret which particular spring holds the key to youth eternal. You might ponder the question as you picnic, hike, or meditate on the banks of Glen Julia Springs. Or think it over as you don snorkeling or scuba equipment and search the underwater caves and crevices of Natural Bridge Spring. Or gently muse while paddling your canoe on Wacissa Springs.

Sinks aren't as inviting as springs, probably because they've been known to open up suddenly and swallow houses, cars, and campers. But the same conditions that create legendary springs also create sinks.

If you could stand on Florida soil and reach deep underground, your fingers would touch layers of clay, limestone, rock, and finally, a limestone cap. Beneath this cap, water may collect, build up pressure, and sometimes force its way to the surface. When this happens, you've got yourself a spring. In contrast, when water dissolves enough limestone to create underground caverns that then collapse, presto, a sinkhole. Vast or small, dry or wet, sinkholes occur in a variety of forms. If the normal channel of drainage becomes blocked, a full-sized lake may form.

But, like bathtubs, sinkhole lakes drain very quickly if the "stopper" is pulled. Alachua Sink was a lake 120 years ago. Great paddlewheel steamers carried commercial cargos and travelers from shore to shore. Then suddenly, in 1891, the plug was pulled, and within hours the steamers were stranded on the bottom like great floundering fish. More recently, the water level at Winter Park sinkhole fell 20 feet in 9 minutes. Winter Park is famous because the earth collapsed suddenly and devoured a home, a pool, and an assortment of motor vehicles in 1981. Another sinkhole collapse took an entire Porche dealership. In areas where sinkholes are common—in central and northern areas of the state—residents often invest in sinkhole insurance. 🐌

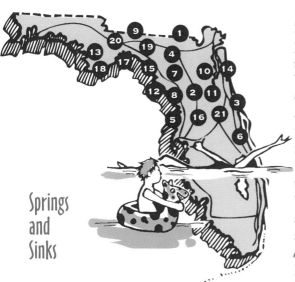

Springs and Sinks

1) Alapaha Rise: This first magnitude spring pumps out 400 million gallons of water each day. The water is carmel colored from tanin, and the area is undeveloped. *FYI:* near Live Oak, at the intersection of US90 and US129.

2) Alexander Springs: This is a first magnitude spring where you can swim, canoe, or hike. *FYI:* Ocala National Forest off SR445; 904-669-3522.

3) Blue Spring State Park: Botanist John Bartram praised this area in his 1766 report to the British Crown just three years after its acquisition from Spain. Endangered manatees winter here in the 72-degree water. You can swim, too, or canoe in Blue Spring Run, or boat and fish on the St. John's River. *FYI:* Orange City; 904-775-3663.

4) Branford Springs: Adjacent to the Suwannee River, the main pool at Branford Springs is 9 feet deep and measures 60 feet in diameter. Swimming, snorkeling, scuba, and dive shop. *FYI:* Branford; 904-776-2748.

5) Chassahowitska Springs: This is a first magnitude spring—the headwaters of the Chassahowitzka River where you can swim, boat, and snorkel. Good largemouth bass fishing in the area. *FYI:* 6 miles south of Homosassa Springs on US19, then west on SR480.

Wakulla Springs boat tour

Wakulla Lodge and Conference Center at Wakulla Springs State Park was built by financier Edward Ball in 1937. The center is now operated by Florida State University's Center for Professional Development. The lodge offers guests a comfortable dose of nostalgia as well as lovely rooms and private marble bathrooms. *FYI:* 14 miles from Tallahassee on SR267; 904-224-5950.

6) De León Springs: 19,000 gallons of water flow from this second magnitude spring each day. Swim, canoe, hike, or make-your-own pancakes courtesy of the Old Spanish Sugar Mill Restaurant. *FYI:* 904-985-4212.

7) Devils Millhopper State Geological Site: Hike via the boardwalk to an ancient sink with its own unique ecosystem. *FYI:* near Gainesville; 904-336-2008.

8) Ginnie Springs: Scuba and diving are popular activities in this 200 foot by 30 foot by 25-foot-deep pool. FYI: High Springs; 904-454-2202.

9) Glen Julia Springs: 200 foot by 100 foot swimming pool. *FYI:* Mount Pleasant.

10) Ichetucknee Springs State Park: 233 million gallons of water bubble from this series of springs each day, and the head spring is a National Natural Landmark. The Ichetucknee River flows for 6 miles before it joins the Santa Fe River. Canoeing, restricted tubing, swimming, and hiking await you. *FYI:* 4 miles northwest of Fort White; 904-497-2511.

11) Juniper Springs: In the 1930s, the Civilian Conservation Corps

carved this pool in natural rock. Swim, sunbathe, picnic, or canoe.
FYI: Ocala National Forest; 904-625-3147.

12) Manatee Springs: Roughly 116.9 million gallons of water flow from the springs each day. Ash, gum, cypress, and maple trees provide shade. Both hammock and sandhill communities are found inside the park. Once the springs join the Suwannee River, they flow 23 miles to the Gulf of Mexico. The spring is named for the endangered manatee rarely seen here. *FYI:* at the end of SR320, west of Chiefland; 904-493-6072.

13) Natural Bridge Spring: Here are first magnitude waters, sinkholes, and a natural bridge where the St. Mark's River goes below ground. This is also a Civil War site. *FYI:* Natural Bridge State Historic Site; 904-925-6216.

14) O'Leno State Park: There are sinkholes galore here along the banks of the Santa Fe River, which vanishes underground for more than 3 miles and reappears magically. Thank the CCC and their development efforts in the 1930s for many park facilities, including the Civilian Conservation Corp bridge. Horseback and hiking trails as well as canoeing, fishing, swimming, and group camp cabins. *FYI:* north of High Springs; 904-454-1853.

15) Peacock Springs State Recreation Area: Thank the Florida Nature Conservancy for these two extensive springs and one of the longest submarine cave systems in the continental U.S. *FYI:* east of Luraville; 904-776-2194.

16) Silver Springs: Commercially developed springs where mastodons used to wade. Swim, golf, pet the animals, or take a cruise in the glass-bottom boat. *FYI:* Silver Springs; 904-236-2121.

17) Spring Creek Springs: These first magnitude springs release below sea level in a tidal marsh. *FYI:* Spring Creek on Oyster Bay.

18) St. Mark's Spring: An undeveloped first magnitude spring in the St. Mark's River. *FYI:* east of Woodville on Natural Bridge Road.

19) Troy Springs: This is a local spot for swimming and scuba diving. The hull of the steamboat Madison, a Confederate Civil War relic, is submerged here. *FYI:* northwest of Branford on the Suwannee River.

20) Wakulla Springs State Park: This is the world's deepest and biggest freshwater spring, where you can swim, snorkel, and cruise via glass-bottom boat or riverboat. The park includes 1,500 acres of upland hardwoods. *Creature from the Black Lagoon* was filmed in the area. *FYI:* 14 miles south of Tallahassee on SR 267; 904-922-3632.

21) Wekiwa Springs State Park: These are the headwaters of Wekiwa River. Swim, canoe, horseback ride. *FYI:* near Apopka; 407-884-2009.

Spirit Yourself Away

Can you "feel" it? The 100-year-old cottages and clipped picket fences of **Cassadaga** give it the feel of a different era, if not a different world. Since 1875, this village has been a psychic mecca and Florida's capital for the spiritual set. Founder and spiritualist George P. Colby chose Cassadaga as the spot to further his ideal of religious freedom. Of course, he didn't choose without help. Three spirits—The Philosopher, The Unknown, and Seneca—acted as otherworldly realtors and gave him the spiritual thumb's up. Here Colby established his **Southern Cassadaga Spirtualist Camp**, and his followers still believe the word of the great religious teachers—Buddha, Jesus, Zoroaster.

Walk the streets of Cassadaga past Healing Tree, up Medium Walk, to near Spirit Pond and you'll see lots of "sisters," "reverends," and "doctors" fronting the names on the mailboxes. Not just anyone can begin practicing as a medium here; prospective spiritualists must complete hours of training and testing before the community will approve a license. More than half of Cassadagas 300 residents are involved in the spiritual medium.

Appropriately, someone at The Book Store will tell you who's "reading" on any given day. Don't expect any dark energy; Cassadaga psychics specialize in positive, upbeat readings. The Spiritualist Church offers weekly services. Seminars are offered at different times of the year. *FYI:* Off I-4 a few miles north of Deltona.

Cassadaga is one of Florida's meccas for the spiritual set

Inner World

If you close your eyes, use your imagination, and take a deep breath at the **Koreshan State Historic Site**, you might get a glimpse of Cyrus Reed Teed's "New Jerusalem." Teed was a religious visionary who led his followers out of Chicago in 1894, and they settled on the banks of Florida's Estero River. Teed envisioned a megacity of ten million people all practicing the religion known as Koreshanity. According to Teed, the world was a hollow sphere, and all living things as well as the planets, moon, sun, and stars were encased within. When Teed died in 1908, the followers of Koreshan dwindled, and the last four members deeded this property to the state in 1961. Nature is the religion here now: fish, boat, picnic, and camp in this lovely setting. *FYI:* US41 at Corkscrew Road; 813-992-0311.

Florida State Archives

The globe showing that we live inside the earth

Middens and Mounds

Around 5,000 B.C., Florida's early aboriginal residents might have played their own "shell game." They certainly used shells as multipurpose instruments. Shell scrapers removed flesh from cuticles, meat from hides, bark from wood. Shell lathes transformed tree trunks into dugout canoes. Shell containers held berries, seeds, and water. Shell jewelry beautified. And, eventually, shells were heaped high with other refuse in piles archaeologists call "middens." Researchers who like to get their hands dirty use middens as timelines, working down from recent innovations like smoking pipes and ornaments, back to pottery shards and spear tips.

Before Jesus was preaching his gospel, Florida's aboriginal cultures had adopted a new trend—burial mounds—to memorialize ancient VIPs. At the center of each mound, a body was buried facing the sun. Other bodies (perhaps family members) were placed face down above the primary body. Finally, a top layer of haphazard bones and bits may have belonged to sacrificial victims—animal and human. Effigies of clay and wood were also scattered throughout the mound.

Burial mounds are thought to have originated with the Hopewell cultures of Illinois and the Ohio River Valley. Perhaps, along with shells and feathers, ideas were swapped between Florida cultures and those to the north. By the first century A.D., burial mounds had evolved into massive earthworks whose significance still puzzles us modern folks. *FYI:* Indian Temple Mound, Fort Walton; 904-243-6521; Lake Jackson Indian Mounds, near Tallahassee; 904-562-0042.

High Blooms

The gardens at **Maclay State Gardens** were created by Alfred and Louise Maclay after they purchased the land in 1923. Louise Maclay designed the public ornamental garden in her husband's memory after his death in 1944. High blooming season is January through April 10. Peak floral days are in mid-March. *FYI:* 1/2 mile north of I-10 on US319; 904-487-4556.

The lush and tropical **Eden State Gardens** surround a historic Gulf Coast home that once belonged to a lumber magnate. Tours and picnic area. *FYI:* Point Washington, CR395; 904-231-4214.

Thank nature for the cut of the land at **Ravine State Gardens**—a steep ravine forged by the waters of St. Johns River—and bless the Works Progress Administration (WPA) for the gardens they created in 1933. Peak flowering season is March through April; coincides with the **Palatka Azalea Festival**. *FYI:* Palatka; 904-329-3721.

Washington Oak State Gardens are bounded by the Atlantic Ocean and the Matanzas River. This 389-acre park offers visitors a chance to unwind, hike, picnic, fish, or stroll through the ornamental gardens. Beach erosion and Coquina rock make for a distinctive coastline. *FYI:* Palm Coast; 904-445-3161.

For a slightly different flavor, stop at **Florida Cactus, Inc.**, on your way to Plymouth. The greenhouses are filled with prickly beauties from every state. There's even a cactus clock. *FYI:* Plymouth via US441.

Florida Dept. of Commerce

Cypress Gardens is famous for its water-skiers, as well as its flora

Ex-pirate John Gomez (1778-1900)

T his legendary former cabin boy to infamous pirate Jose Gaspar eventually became a pirate in his own right—and took a turn as well at Indian fighter, hunter, woodsman, farmer, guide, resort operator, fisherman, and, during the Civil War, ship's pilot.

"Old John" Gomez was probably born on the island of Madeira and then transplanted to Spain in time to see Napoleon strut his stuff. As an adolescent he was captured during an ocean voyage by the pirate Gaspar (Gasparilla). After Gasparilla's ship was incapacitated by a U.S. warship, Gomez escaped the hangman's noose by swimming to the pirate's den on Gasparilla Island at Boca Grande.

His luck turned when he met a kind widow, Sara Shavers, to whom he was happily married until Sara's death in the 1850s. A scandal with a second widow caused Gomez to report that another suitor had "come 'long the road. I take my gun. I say, Willums, I no wanta you come in here. He say, I come in, I killa you. I say, Willums, donta come in da gate. Willums, he coma in da gate. I shoota him, and he staya there. I coma 'way."

(Very) Old John settled on Panther Key (now Gomez Key) and fished and farmed and married again, until his accidental death by drowning—at age 122. 🐌

The Last of the Pirates: John Gomez, a.k.a. Panther Key John

Florida State Archives

In the heydey of Florida's pirates, Gasparilla Island was a hideout

Pirate Trivia Quiz

1) Pirate José Gaspar supposedly sank ___ ships within 11 years.
a) 8 **b)** 36 **c)** 90

2) When his pirate ship was mortally damaged by a U.S. warship, Gaspar _____.
a) surrendered **b)** went down with his ship **c)** wrapped himself in the anchor and jumped overboard to his death

3) When a young naval surgeon, Odette Phillippe, successfully treated a group of sick pirates, pirate John Gomez gave him

_____.

a) a treasure chest filled with gold **b)** an island **c)** safe passage to French territory

Answers:
1) b 2) c 3) a

The possibilities of a Bermuda Triangle government cover-up, top-secret research, and an alien loading zone have all been explored in numerous books, articles, and television shows.

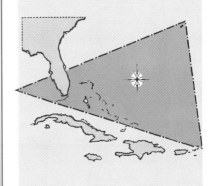

An English spy's drawing of a Spanish treasure frigate prior to 1588

Lost Treasure

Quivira was a city where the streets were paved with gold and people drank from golden goblets and bathed in golden tubs. At least, that's what ancient legends tell us. Florida has its share of newer legends, many of which deal with buried or sunken treasure. According to one professional salvager, in the Florida Keys alone, there's a shipwreck for every quarter mile of water. There's no question that treasures worth 20, 30, and 40 million dollars have been salvaged from Florida waters already.

1) Indian Key: In the late 1700s, the salvage industry flourished on the Florida Keys as commerce ships navigated the Gulf Stream and Bahama Channel, risking close proximity to submerged and deadly coral reefs. In 1831, Jacob Housman bought Indian Key as a base for his wrecking business. Warehouses, wharves, and a hotel served visitors and a resident population of about 70 people. But on August 7, 1840, Seminole Indians leveled the town to ashes when they heard of Housman's plans to offer a bounty for their heads. Today, access by private or charter boat only; boat tours leave from Indian Key. *FYI:* Islamorada; 305-664-4815.

2) San Pedro Underwater Archaeological Preserve: Although you won't find treasure on board, the San Pedro was part of the fleet

Treasure, Sunken and Otherwise

of New Spain, and it did go down in 1733. In 1960, the wreck of this 287-ton Dutch-made ship was discovered 18 feet down in Hawk Channel near Indian Key. Salvaging took most of it, but you can explore a pile of ballast stones. Those cannons and the anchor are replicas—and so is the information plaque—as if you hadn't guessed. *FYI:* 1.25 nautical miles south from Indian Key at LORAN coordinates 14082.1 and 43320.6; 305-664-4815.

3) The McLarty Treasure Museum: This is located on the site of a Spanish salvor's camp, and it gives treasure buffs a comprehensive look at the history of the 1715 Treasure Fleet. The museum is part of **Sebastian Inlet State Recreation Area**. Certified and only certified scuba divers can explore the Atlantic for gold. *FYI:* on A1A, Melbourne Beach; 407-984-4852.

4) Fisher's Treasure Salvors, Inc.: Mel Fisher is treasure-hunting king when it comes to sunken 16th- and 17th-century Spanish ships. In 1960, Fisher vowed to find the wrecks of the war galleons the Atocha and the Santa Margarita, which went down in the Straits of Florida—treasure-laden according to rumors—during a 1622 hurricane. After toil and tragedy, Fisher found the Atocha in June 1971. You can buy T-shirts and books here, but booty-viewing is reserved for big-time investors. *FYI:* 425 Caroline St., Key West.

5) Naples Beach: If you prefer your treasure on dry land—bring your shovel and your metal detector—check out Florida's West Coast. In fact, L. Frank Hudson diagrams pirate tree markings in his book *Lost Treasure of Florida's Gulf Coast.*

6) The 9-foot **Christ of the Deep Statue** is submerged in 20 feet of water at Key Largo Dry Rocks. This is a favorite of divers.

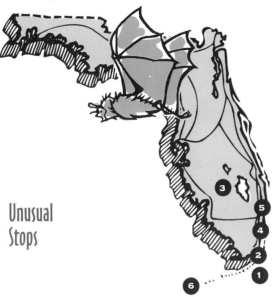

**Unusual
Stops**

One of a Kind

**1) Jule's Undersea
Lodge:** Inside Key Largo
Undersea Park, at Jules'
Undersea Lodge, you and
five friends can relax in
your bed chamber some
30 feet beneath the sea.
The Mermaid Service and
the ocean view might be
worth the price, but let's
face it, we're talking nov-
elty here. *FYI:* 305-451-
2353.

2) Coral Castle: For two
decades, Ed Leedskalnin
mined, hauled, and carved 1,110 tons of coral until he created Coral
Castle. There's a 30-ton Polaris telescope balanced on the north wall.
But that's not all; there's a throne, fountains, and a 9-ton gate. *FYI:*
near Homestead AFB.

Florida Dept. of Commerce

Guests at Jule's Undersea Lodge

3) Cypress Knee Museum: The signs lure you in like a hungry fish: "What's your cypress knee I.Q.?" Since 1934, Tom Gaskins has been collecting cypress knees that brought to mind animals, faces, and even body parts. Check out FDR and Donald Duck. *FYI:* near Palmdale via US27.

4) Parrot Jungle and Gardens: This is a preserve for free-roaming birds such as macaws, parrots, cockatoos, and flamingos. There are parrot shows in the Parrot Bowl Theater—yes, they sing, talk, roller-skate, and ride mini-scooters. *FYI:* 57th Ave. off US1 south, Miami.

5) Butterfly World: Incredible butterflies flutter around this unique museum, botanical garden, and farm. *FYI:* off the Florida Turnpike, Coconut Creek.

6) You've seen the signs in every tourist town, U.S.A.: "Oldest House!" "Oldest Tree!" "Oldest Church!" That's where couples often stop to catch a celluloid memory. When you're in Key West, you might join the masses and snap a few shots of the "**Southernmost House**" or the "**Southernmost Point**" (which resembles a large, overturned thimble). That's Southernmost in the Continental U.S. 🐚

KIDS' ADVENTURES

There are two schools of thought when it comes to Florida's theme parks: 1) They are a blight on the environment; 2) They are the best invention since sliced bread. Kids (of all ages) almost always vote for #2. If you want theme parks, head for Orlando, the theme park capital of the world. Heavy-duty theme fans, bear in mind you need days, days, and more days to explore it all. Oh, yes . . . you need money, too.

Walt Disney World: Epcot Center

Twice the size of Manhattan, "the World" is the world's largest commercial (ultra-commercial) tourist attraction. It has 25 million visitors each year—they spend $2 billion dollars—and a staff of 26,000 (making it the state's largest nongovernment employer).

Epcot Center—complete with **The Living Seas**, **Spaceship Earth**, **Universe of Energy**, **World of Motion**, and **Wonders of Life**—offers educationally oriented exhibits and activities. They're fun and interesting, but they can't compete with the Magic Kingdom.

At the **Magic Kingdom**, **Space Mountain** is the number one attraction. Although the ride lasts less than three minutes—and the wait feels like three hours—it's worth standing in line. In fact, some kids do it over and over again.

The **Jungle Cruise** lets young kids experience the thrill of a deep, dark jungle boat ride while grown-ups may enjoy the plant species on view. Below a certain age, you don't notice the wiring.

Pirates of the Caribbean is a fairy tale boat ride past dioramas featuring unsavory characters. Since 10,000 pirates used to roam Florida and Caribbean waters, it doesn't seem all that far-fetched.

At the **Haunted House**, you're surrounded by ghosts—courtesy of hologram technology. This is one experience old and young will not forget. *FYI:* 407-824-4321.

Universal Studios Florida is the largest Orlando tourist attraction independent of Walt Disney World. This is a cousin of Hollywood, California's studio tour. Special effects are the thing here. King Kong wreaks havoc, a giant shark snaps its massive jaws, and the San Francisco earthquake leaves survivors trembling. *FYI:* International Drive; 407-363-8000.

Florida Dept. of Commerce.

*This six-ton Kong is part of Kongfrontation at **Universal Studios**, Orlando*

For lovers of sun and surf, Florida offers more than 8,000 miles of shoreline

Florida State Parks

The entire state of Florida is dotted with **state parks**, and each offers special events during the year. The activities listed below are great fun for kids of all ages as well as adults. Do call ahead; programs are subject to change, and there are additional events to choose from. A complete listing of state parks is available from the Department of Natural Resources, Division of Recreation and Parks, MS #535, 3900 Commonwealth Blvd., Tallahassee, FL 32399-3000.

Annual Manatee Springs Fall Festival: Arts and crafts demonstrations and exhibits, Seminole Indians in authentic dress, living history camps, food, square dancing, and riverboat rides are all part of the fun in October. *FYI:* Manatee Springs State Park; 904-493-6072.

Moonlight Canoe Trips: Explore nature under the light of the full moon on a ranger-guided excursion. Reservations are required for these seasonal trips. *FYI:* Ichetucknee Springs State Park; 904-497-2511.

Santa's Village of Christmas Past: A craft show, horse-drawn carriage rides, pontoon boat tours, caroling, and a recreated Victorian holiday village are all part of the festivities. *FYI:* Koreshan State Historic Site; 813-992-0311.

Tunes in the Dunes: Fun, music, and a festive spirit are all part of this annual September event. This is part of the national coastal cleanup, and big and little hands are welcome. *FYI:* St. George Island State Park; 904-927-2111.

1876 Cow Camp: Learn about the cow hunter's life, and meet Florida Cracker cattle descended from stock brought by Spanish explorers. Pack a picnic lunch for this annual fall event. *FYI:* Lake Kissimmee State Park; 813-696-1112.

Union Garrison Weekend: This living history display portrays fort life in the 1800s. Marching, saber drills, cannon firing, and smithing are some of the things to be seen in late summer. *FYI:* Fort Clinch State Park.

Beach Walk Turtle Program: Two-hour guided beach walks are offered in the morning several times a week. Learn about sea turtles, and search for signs of turtle nesting sites. Don't forget the sunscreen. *FYI:* Honeymoon Island State Recreation Area; 813-469-5942.

Shelling: Kids love shelling, and a ranger-guided expedition on an island accessible only by boat is the perfect way to learn shell basics and expand expertise. *FYI:* Cayo Costa State Park; 813-964-0375.

Long Key Day: Canoe races and snorkeling instruction are offered as part of this annual event each July. You must bring your own snorkel gear, sunscreen, and camera (optional). *FYI:* Long Key State Recreation Area; 305-664-4815. ₰

INDEX

Other Books from John Muir Publications

Asia Through the Back Door, 4th ed., 400 pp. $16.95 (available 7/93)

Belize: A Natural Destination, 336 pp. $16.95

Costa Rica: A Natural Destination, 2nd ed., 310 pp. $16.95

Elderhostels: The Students' Choice, 2nd ed., 304 pp. $15.95

Environmental Vacations: Volunteer Projects to Save the Planet, 2nd ed., 248 pp. $16.95

Europe 101: History & Art for the Traveler, 4th ed., 350 pp. $15.95

Europe Through the Back Door, 11th ed., 432 pp. $17.95

Europe Through the Back Door Phrase Book: French, 160 pp. $4.95

Europe Through the Back Door Phrase Book: German, 160 pp. $4.95

Europe Through the Back Door Phrase Book: Italian, 168 pp. $4.95

Europe Through the Back Door Phrase Book: Spanish & Portuguese, 288 pp. $4.95

A Foreign Visitor's Guide to America, 224 pp. $12.95

Great Cities of Eastern Europe, 256 pp. $16.95

Guatemala: A Natural Destination, 336 pp. $16.95

Indian America: A Traveler's Companion, 4th ed., 448 pp. $17.95 (available 7/93)

Interior Furnishings Southwest, 256 pp. $19.95

Mona Winks: Self-Guided Tours of Europe's Top Museums, 2nd ed., 448 pp. $16.95

Opera! The Guide to Western Europe's Great Houses, 296 pp. $18.95

Paintbrushes and Pistols: How the Taos Artists Sold the West, 288 pp. $17.95

The People's Guide to Mexico, 9th ed., 608 pp. $18.95

Ranch Vacations: The Complete Guide to Guest and Resort, Fly-Fishing, and Cross-Country Skiing Ranches, 2nd ed., 396 pp. $18.95

The Shopper's Guide to Art and Crafts in the Hawaiian Islands, 272 pp. $13.95

The Shopper's Guide to Mexico, 224 pp. $9.95

Understanding Europeans, 272 pp. $14.95

Undiscovered Islands of the Caribbean, 3rd ed., 288 pp. $14.95

Undiscovered Islands of the Mediterranean, 2nd ed., 224 pp. $13.95

Undiscovered Islands of the U.S. and Canadian West Coast, 288 pp. $12.95

Unique Colorado, 112 pp. $10.95 (available 6/93)

Unique Florida, 112 pp. $10.95 (available 7/93)

Unique New Mexico, 112 pp. $10.95 (available 6/93)

A Viewer's Guide to Art: A Glossary of Gods, People, and Creatures, 144 pp. $10.95

The Visitor's Guide to the Birds of the Eastern National Parks: United States and Canada, 410 pp. $15.95

2 to 22 Days Series
Each title offers 22 flexible daily itineraries useful for planning vacations of any length. Aside from valuable general information, included are "must see" attractions *and* hidden "jewels."

2 to 22 Days in the American Southwest, 1993 ed., 176 pp. $10.95

2 to 22 Days in Asia, 1993 ed., 176 pp. $9.95

2 to 22 Days in Australia, 1993 ed., 192 pp. $9.95

2 to 22 Days in California, 1993 ed., 192 pp. $9.95

2 to 22 Days in Europe, 1993 ed., 288 pp. $13.95

2 to 22 Days in Florida, 1993 ed., 192 pp. $10.95

2 to 22 Days in France, 1993 ed., 192 pp. $10.95

2 to 22 Days in Germany, Austria, & Switzerland, 1993 ed., 224 pp. $10.95

2 to 22 Days in Great Britain, 1993 ed., 192 pp. $10.95

2 to 22 Days Around the Great Lakes, 1993 ed., 192 pp. $10.95

2 to 22 Days in Hawaii, 1993 ed., 192 pp. $9.95

2 to 22 Days in Italy, 208 pp. $10.95

2 to 22 Days in New England, 1993 ed., 192 pp. $10.95

2 to 22 Days in New Zealand, 1993 ed., 192 pp. $9.95

2 to 22 Days in Norway, Sweden, & Denmark, 1993 ed., 192 pp. $10.95

2 to 22 Days in the Pacific Northwest, 1993 ed., 192 pp. $10.95

2 to 22 Days in the Rockies, 1993 ed., 192 pp. $10.95

2 to 22 Days in Spain & Portugal, 192 pp. $10.95

2 to 22 Days in Texas, 1993 ed., 192 pp. $9.95

2 to 22 Days in Thailand, 1993 ed., 180 pp. $9.95

22 Days (or More) Around the World, 1993 ed., 264 pp. $12.95

Automotive Titles

How to Keep Your VW Alive, 15th ed., 464 pp. $21.95

How to Keep Your Subaru Alive 480 pp. $21.95

How to Keep Your Toyota Pickup Alive 392 pp. $21.95

How to Keep Your Datsun/Nissan Alive 544 pp. $21.95

The Greaseless Guide to Car Care Confidence, 224 pp. $14.95

Off-Road Emergency Repair & Survival, 160 pp. $9.95

TITLES FOR YOUNG READERS AGES 8 AND UP

"Kidding Around" Travel Guides for Young Readers
All the "Kidding Around" Travel guides are 64 pages and $9.95 paper, except for **Kidding Around Spain** and **Kidding Around the National Parks of the Southwest**, which are 108 pages and $12.95 paper.

Kidding Around Atlanta
Kidding Around Boston, 2nd ed.
Kidding Around Chicago, 2nd ed.
Kidding Around the Hawaiian Islands
Kidding Around London
Kidding Around Los Angeles
Kidding Around the National Parks of the Southwest
Kidding Around New York City, 2nd ed.
Kidding Around Paris
Kidding Around Philadelphia
Kidding Around San Diego
Kidding Around San Francisco
Kidding Around Santa Fe
Kidding Around Seattle
Kidding Around Spain
Kidding Around Washington, D.C., 2nd ed.

"Extremely Weird" Series for Young Readers. Written by Sarah Lovett, each is 48 pages and $9.95

Extremely Weird Bats
Extremely Weird Birds
Extremely Weird Endangered
Species
Extremely Weird Fishes
Extremely Weird Frogs
Extremely Weird Insects
Extremely Weird Mammals
(available 8/93)
Extremely Weird Micro Monsters
(available 8/93)
Extremely Weird Primates
Extremely Weird Reptiles
Extremely Weird Sea Creatures
Extremely Weird Snakes (available 8/93)
Extremely Weird Spiders

"Masters of Motion" Series for Young Readers. Each title is 48 pages and $9.95 paper.
How to Drive an Indy Race Car
How to Fly a 747
How to Fly the Space Shuttle

"X-ray Vision" Series for Young Readers. Each title is 48 pages and $9.95 paper.
Looking Inside Cartoon Animation
Looking Inside Sports Aerodynamics
Looking Inside the Brain
Looking Inside Sunken Treasure
Looking Inside Telescopes and the Night Sky

Multicultural Titles for Young Readers
Native Artists of North America, 48 pp. $14.95 hardcover
The Indian Way: Learning to Communicate with Mother Earth, 114 pp. $9.95
The Kids' Environment Book: What's Awry and Why, 192 pp. $13.95
Kids Explore America's African-American Heritage, 112 pp. $8.95
Kids Explore America's Hispanic Heritage, 112 pp. $7.95

Environmental Titles for Young Readers
Rads, Ergs, and Cheeseburgers: The Kids' Guide to Energy and the Environment, 108 pp. $12.95
Habitats: Where the Wild Things Live, 48 pp. $9.95
The Kids' Environment Book: What's Awry and Why, 192 pp. $13.95

Ordering Information
Please check your local bookstore for our books, or call 1-800-888-7504 to order direct from us. All orders are shipped via UPS; see chart below to calculate your shipping charge to U.S. destinations. **No P.O. Boxes please; we must have a street address to ensure delivery.** If the book you request is not available, we will hold your check until we can ship it. Foreign orders will be shipped surface rate unless otherwise requested; please enclose $3.00 for the first item and $1.00 for each additional item.

For U.S. Orders Totaling	Add
Up to $15.00	$4.25
$15.01 to $45.00	$5.25
$45.01 to $75.00	$6.25
$75.01 or more	$7.25

Methods of Payment
Check, money order, American Express, MasterCard, or Visa. We cannot be responsible for cash sent through the mail. For credit card orders, include your card number, expiration date, and your signature, or call (800) 888-7504. American Express card orders can be shipped only to billing address of cardholder. Sorry, no C.O.D.'s. Residents of sunny New Mexico, add 6.125% tax to total.

Address all orders and inquiries to:
John Muir Publications
P.O. Box 613
Santa Fe, NM 87504
(505) 982-4078
(800) 888-7504